KU-115-495

MABON

William Abraham

MABON

(WILLIAM ABRAHAM 1842-1922)

A Study in Trade Union Leadership

By

E. W. Evans

Preface by
PROFESSOR A. BEACHAM

CARDIFF
UNIVERSITY OF WALES PRESS
1959

Mawr wron llafur, marworyn llwyfan,
Dawnus ei enaid, hynaws ei anian,
Anwylyn dewraf, i'n hawliau'n darian,
A glân weledydd o galon lydan.
   O'i dal dŵr dihidlai dân—dros y gwir,
A'i hwyl a gofir gan genedl gyfan.

Dyfed

PRINTED BY THE CAMBRIAN NEWS LTD.

UNIVERSITY COLLEGE LIBRARY SWANSEA

SOUTH WALES MINERS LIBRARY

TO
MY PARENTS

ACKNOWLEDGEMENTS

IT would be impossible to enumerate every person who contributed towards this study. But I remain very greatly indebted to all the veteran colliers and others who interested themselves in my problems.

I am especially grateful to Mrs. Rachel Williams, of London, and to Mr. Mabon Abraham, of Cardiff, for their kindness in allowing me to read such of Mabon's personal papers as had survived the years. And also to the officials of the National Union of Mine-workers at Cardiff, for giving me every facility in consulting the records of their organisation.

In ordering the material I received helpful criticism from Mr. J. H. Morris and Mr. L. J. Williams of the Department of Economics, Aberystwyth. Professor David Williams of the Department of Modern Welsh History also devoted many hours to reading and correcting the early drafts, to my very great advantage. My debt to Professor Arthur Beacham of the Department of Economics, Aberystwyth, cannot adequately be expressed. This work was begun under his direction, and but for his help, encouragement and guidance it would never have been completed.

My sincere thanks are due also to the publishers and printers for many valuable suggestions and for their infinite patience.

E.W.E.

Manchester University.

CONTENTS

PREFACE

About seven years ago the late Thomas Jones, C.H., entertained myself and an American Professor to dinner. In the course of the evening ' T.J.' remarked that it was curious that so little work had been done within the University of Wales on the industrial history of South Wales during the nineteenth century. He even took it upon himself to wonder what Professors of Economics in the University did with their time and thought that perhaps a special responsibility lay upon that particular Professor who laboured in the shadow of the National Library of Wales.

The hint was taken as he knew it would be. A good deal of work on the economic history of South Wales was started during the next few years (mainly, but not only, at Aberystwyth), some of which has already been published. The main effort was concentrated on general studies of particular industries but it was also hoped to produce from time to time more specialised studies of the great men of the period, of particular firms, associations and so on. Dr. Eric Wyn Evans started work on William Abraham in 1952 and submitted an M.A. thesis on this subject in 1953. Preparation of the work for publication in book form has been held up by Dr. Evans' spell of duty in the West Indies as Lecturer in the University College at Kingston. My own part in it as supervisor of the research has been very slight. If I was able to evoke occasionally for Dr. Evans something of the atmosphere of the period as I had learned of it from my grandfather and his five coal-sodden sons I have been well rewarded by the results of his researches as they are here presented.

' T.J.' would have been pleased that our first biographical study should be of Mabon. To men of Tom Jones' outlook and generation Mabon was typical of the truly heroic period of trade unionism. That was a time when union leaders were expected to lead and did so. The truths which they expounded were the simple truths of the New Testament and not the tortuous canon of Karl Marx. In their lives and by their example they sought to show that the better wages and conditions for which they fought were means to a better life and not more beer and skittles.

Mabon's gifts appear to have been those of oratory and leadership rather than the ability to think out difficult problems of union structure and policy. But for the time in which he lived he was just about right. And there was a simple directness about his thinking which might not have taken him so far astray today. He would have responded readily to pleas for better treatment for unemployed miners. He would have roundly rejected pleas to close the open-casts, restrict the use of oil, and stop the atomic power stations. Anything which limited the need to labour in the darkness and the dust would have seemed pure gain to him. Yet it will be said by those who read this book that Mabon had notable defects as a miners' leader and that these became more obvious as time went on. Perhaps so. His greatest 'defect' is common to most of us. Times and circumstances changed but he did not.

I hope that this book will bring pleasure to many who have worked or are working in the coal industry. My students, my colleagues and myself owe much to many such who have helped with this and other research. To others we hope that it will communicate something more than the filth and squalor that have been so much emphasised in the history of coal. The rise of South Wales to industrial greatness was not an insignificant episode in our history. There is much to be told which can still excite the blood and quicken the pulse. The names of men like Powell, Lewis, and Williams (on the owners' side) or those of Abraham, Brace and Richards (on the men's side) deserve to be inscribed in the annals of the Welsh people no less than those of the poets and preachers we hear so much more about.

A. BEACHAM.

MABON

A Study in Trade Union Leadership

INTRODUCTION

IT IS remarkable that so little is known of the life and work of William Abraham. During his lifetime he enjoyed a nation-wide reputation, and no name appears more frequently in the history of the South Wales coalfield prior to the first world war. It is true that his influence waned before the end of his life. But this was nothing compared with the oblivion into which William Abraham's name fell after his death. It means nothing to the present generation of miners or, if vaguely familiar, is only associated with the monthly holiday which he instituted in the coalfield over sixty years ago. This holiday, however, was perhaps the least of his achievements. If he is to be remembered at all, it should be for his work in connection with the Eight Hour Day, the Workmen's Compensation Act and, above all, the growth of trade unionism in South Wales.

His efforts in this direction are almost entirely forgotten today. Yet for some forty years he was undoubtedly pre-eminent among the miners' leaders in South Wales, in a period which produced a greater number of outstanding men in this field than has perhaps been seen at any other time. So high was his prestige that for nearly two generations the policy of the miners' organisations was moulded almost entirely by his own outlook on industrial questions. Conciliation and arbitration, which were his solutions to the problem of relationships between employers and men, became the official policy of the South Wales miners' unions in the years of his supremacy. Under the influence of his ideals the mining district of South Wales enjoyed a period of nearly two decades during which no stoppage occurred, for William Abraham abhorred strikes. To appreciate the full significance of this achievement we have only to remember the unenviable reputation which the area subsequently acquired as a storm centre of industrial warfare.

It is no exaggeration to say that the whole development of the miners' organisations bore the unmistakable impress of his views. This was only to be expected, since it was mainly by his untiring efforts that the workmen did, in fact, become organised. For a long time they failed to see the advantages of trade unionism, while he, and often he alone, laboured unceasingly to lay the foundations of a permanent association. By encouraging the development of local organisations he paved the way for the Miners' Federation, from which sprang the powerful union that operates in the coalfield today.

For all these reasons it is obvious that the passing of William Abraham, trade unionist and apostle of industrial peace, marked the end of an era in the South Wales coal industry.

I

EARLY YEARS

IN THE middle of the nineteenth century the village of Cwmavon, near Port Talbot, was very little different from many others in South Wales that had felt the impact of the new industrialism. The presence of coal seams, which were worked from about 1750, had attracted both iron and copper smelting industries to the area. As the industrial development gathered momentum the village had grown rapidly to accommodate the miners and metal-workers drawn in from the surrounding countryside.

Along with the new industries came Methodism. The ancient church of St. Michael continued to serve successive generations as it had done in the past, but the religious temper of Cwmavon at this time was predominantly non-conformist. Howell Harris, John Wesley and William Williams all visited the district, and the meetings held at private houses had led to the building of many chapels by various denominations during the early nineteenth century.

Into this environment of industrial activity and non-conformist tradition William Abraham was born on 14 June, 1842, the fourth son of Thomas and Mary Abraham. Little is known of his early years, but a few facts can be established with reasonable certainty. His father was a native of Llanfabon who had removed to Cwmavon early in life. By occupation he was both collier and copper-smelter, and probably alternated between these trades according to their relative prosperity. No more is known of Thomas Abraham, however, and it was undoubtedly the influence of his mother that dominated the formative years of the future labour leader. Evidently Mary Abraham was not only deeply religious but also hard-working, intelligent and fairly well educated by contemporary standards. The death of her husband at an early age left her with the care of a large family. Nevertheless, she contrived to maintain an

1

excellent home for her children and, in the words of her son,
' never weakened in her efforts to plant in their minds the
principles of true devotion.'[1] Her teaching and conduct undoubtedly made a lasting impression upon him, inculcating
the essential principles of Christian belief which were later to
mould his attitude towards industrial issues.

The National School at Cwmavon provided him with a
rudimentary knowledge of reading, writing and arithmetic,
but it cannot be claimed that he ever attained a high standard
of education in an academic sense. His formal schooling of
necessity ended when he started work as a door-boy in the
mines at the age of ten. But the familiarity which he showed in
later years with the works of John Stuart Mill, Carlyle and
Tennyson, as well as of Ceiriog and other Welsh writers,
suggests that he read widely. Further, he improved his education through the facilities offered by the many aspects of chapel
life which were open to him. In his own words, ' What I am
today, whatever that may be, I owe to the Sunday School, the
Band of Hope and to the Eisteddfod.'[2] This was perhaps an
exaggeration, but the essays and poetry for which he won so
many prizes must at least have increased his command of the
Welsh language. Moreover, it should be remembered that at
this time the course of instruction offered by the Sunday
School was not confined to religious teaching. In many ways it
was complementary to that provided by the day-school, and
was perhaps of higher quality.

His activities within the chapel may be said to have prepared
him for his future career. They gave him self-confidence in
public and developed his powers of oratory ; even his fine
tenor voice, which was trained in these circumstances, was one
day to calm restive audiences and sway the counsels of the
miners. It was within the chapel, indeed, that William Abraham
first emerged as a leader. At fourteen, now a seasoned working
man, he became the leader of the Band of Hope at Tabernacl
Calvinistic Methodist chapel. Two years later he was conducting the choir, and soon after he was himself giving instruction
in the Sunday School. When his skill as a conductor became
known his services were also in demand outside his own

denomination. Under his leadership the choir of the Rock, an Independent chapel, achieved some reputation by its successes at choral festivals throughout the district.

Meanwhile he had worked his way through the various grades of employment in the coalmines. He was probably engaged at one of the pits owned by the Cwmavon works. If this is so, it may help to explain his sympathetic and friendly attitude towards employers in later life, for the employees of this company were exceptionally well-treated. By 1850 the works had passed under the control of the Bank of England, and were managed by John Biddulph, an unusual man who held remarkably enlightened views. Through his influence the company's schools were enlarged, two clergymen engaged to minister to the workmen, and evening classes begun for both men and women. At the same time reading rooms were opened in various parts of the valley, which contained ' an abundance of well-selected books, papers and reviews', and also a Mechanics' Institute. This Institute was used not only for lectures but also for musical entertainments, arranged 'chiefly by young men belonging to the works', who probably included William Abraham. In any case we may assume that he made the fullest use of these facilities, which were perhaps unrivalled in South Wales at this time, to further his education and his knowledge of literature.

The Cwmavon works, moreover, did not neglect the physical well-being of its workmen. Sanitation and refuse collection was organised by the company, a penny in the pound being deducted from wages to meet the expense. The ' company shop ' was closed, and wages were paid monthly in money, with weekly advances available if needed. To counteract the effects of closing this shop a market was opened for the use of private tradesmen, so that prices at Cwmavon were no higher than at Swansea. The company's houses were maintained in excellent condition, and tenants given every incentive to cultivate gardens.[3] As a further precaution Biddulph even restricted the number of beerhouses in the area, although this would not have affected William Abraham, who remained a strict teetotaller for most of his life.

Clearly any workman engaged at the Cwmavon company's pits might be expected to have a more tolerant attitude towards employers than would a miner at almost any other colliery. It is, of course, tempting to believe that William Abraham was influenced in this way, and to explain his views on industrial relations in such terms. But at best this can only be a partial solution. The evidence is not clear, but it seems that he was eventually dismissed by the colliery manager, and found employment at the spelter works nearby. The point is especially interesting because he was discharged, as he put it, for ' upholding the rights of his fellow workmen'.[4] Few of these fellow workmen can have imagined that this seventeen-year-old who was victimised for demanding justice would one day speak for all the miners in South Wales.

Little can be said of William Abraham's years in the spelter works. But a record has been preserved of at least one important event that occurred at this time, namely his marriage at the parish church of Cwmavon on 18 August, 1860. His bride was Sarah, the daughter of Mary and David Williams, the local blacksmith. Both were only nineteen years of age, although Sarah was certainly some months older than her husband, for the church records show that she was baptised on 23 January, 1842. Immediately after the wedding the young couple left for a brief honeymoon at Mumbles, and on their return made their home at Cwmavon. Sarah, like many women of the time, seems to have been denied the advantage of even elementary education, for she signed the marriage certificate by mark. The marriage, however, was completely successful, and she shared as a devoted wife many of her husband's triumphs in later years. Whether he travelled to small meetings and eisteddfodau or dined with Gladstone, Sarah was often his companion until her sudden death at Mumbles on 13 July, 1900. Yet she does not appear to have taken an important part in his public life. She seems to have preferred to remain in the background, a good mother to their twelve children, eight of whom survived infancy, and concerned more with William's home life than with his career.

In 1864 an opportunity arose for William Abraham and

eleven other Welshmen to sail for Chile, where well-paid work was available in the copper mines under a three-year contract.[5] Leaving his wife and two children, he sailed in the *Hawkeye*, and reached Valparaiso after an exciting four months voyage, having rounded the Horn and evaded the Spanish navy's blockade of Peru and Chile. But he found that no work was available, and after a month's idleness he was compelled to accept employment at Tonguoy at relatively low wages. One month later he and five others were moved down the coast to Carazel, but disappointed expectations, homesickness and the separation from Sarah and the children made him resolve to return home. A chance meeting with a Captain Walters, of Truro, gave him an opportunity to work his passage home, and he finally reached Cwmavon after an absence of thirteen months.[6] Immediately on arrival, however, he was called upon by the elders of Tabernacl chapel to account for his having returned before the three-year contract had expired. This is an interesting demonstration of the nonconformist belief in the sanctity of contracts, which helps to explain the firmness with which William Abraham in later years opposed violation of contractual obligations.

Fortunately he was able to resume work at the spelter works through the influence of a friend, so that he lost nothing by his Chilean adventure. But towards the close of the sixties the industry experienced a recession and he, with many others, was put on short time. In the hope of finding steady work he finally accompanied one Evan Daniel and his family when they removed from Cwmavon to Cwmbwrla, near Swansea, in 1869. There he found employment at the tinplate works, of which he remarked later that :

> ' The work was very different from that with which I had become accustomed . . . . It was excessively hard, and needed a man of great strength to do it. We had to break up the iron " stamps" which, after coming from the furnace, had been under the forge hammer. To do this we had to use a great sledge-hammer weighing fifty pounds, and it is to the training which this gave my muscles that I attribute my strength of arm, which remains to the present day.'[7]

Yet despite the exhausting nature of the work he threw himself whole-heartedly into the religious and social life of Babell Calvinistic Methodist chapel, which had recently been built. Soon he was conducting the Babell Glee Party and, as usual, playing a leading part in the Band of Hope. There he also began to build up a reputation as poet and singer. It was during this period that he adopted the *nom de plume* of ' Gwilym Mabon ', which, contracted to ' Mabon', was later to become his best-known title. It has been suggested that he derived it from his father's birthplace, Llanfabon, although Robert Smillie purports to give Mabon's own explanation that he adopted it because it meant ' bard'.[8] If this is so, then Mabon was himself mistaken.

The tinplate industry held no real attraction for Mabon, and in 1870 he returned once again to the coalmines, finding work as a collier in the Caercynydd pit at Waunarlwydd, near Gowerton. This decision to re-enter the mines marks an important turning point in his career. It brought him into contact with the industrial troubles of the period, and placed him in the environment which was to make him a miner's leader and a figure of national importance.

In the coalfields of England the miners had been forming new unions throughout the sixties. Most of these owed nominal allegiance to the Miners' National Union, an organisation set up during 1863. But this body refused to deal with the question of wages or to support strikes, and confined its efforts to the promotion of mining legislation. Many members, however, had come to feel that such an attitude was ridiculous while wage bargaining remained the main function of trade unions. Discontent had grown, until in 1869 a new organisation had been established in Lancashire, known as the Amalgamated Association of Miners. Its avowed purpose was agitation on the question of wages, and, although favouring arbitration as a means of settling disputes, its leaders were not averse to the use of the strike weapon. Already this militant union was sending delegates into South Wales to organise the men. Low wages and the employers' disregard of the anti-truck laws made the Welsh miners willing to support the movement, and it was only a matter of time before the ferment spread to Gowerton.

Meanwhile Mabon's religious life centred around Bethel (Gowerton) and Seion (Waunarlwydd), the latter being a Baptist chapel. It is worth noting that the pastor of Seion, the Reverend William Davies, strongly advised him to enter the ministry, and promised him all possible assistance. Mabon refused, however, despite the fact that his mother, too, hoped to see him ordained. This incident is an interesting confirmation of the rather cynical observation sometimes made that politics, the ministry and trade union leadership all demand the same abilities. But more important, it emphasises the sincerity of Mabon's religious convictions. When in later years he sought to apply Christian principles to the problems of industrial relations it was the course which might be expected of a man who had been judged worthy of the ministry.

During his years at Waunarlwydd, Mabon had built up a widespread reputation as a singer, and was also much sought after as a choir leader at local eisteddfodau. But in the summer of 1871 an event of some importance occurred, which was to bring Mabon before a much larger audience than that of the local eisteddfod. In his own words :

' Lewis Morgan of Treorchy came over to address a meeting at Waunarlwydd on behalf of the Amalgamated Association of Miners. Lewis Morgan was not an eloquent speaker, although he was a thorough master of his subject. He put his case strongly enough, but he spoke in English and seemed to make little impression on the meeting. His address only lasted about twenty minutes, and it seemed likely that the meeting would come to an end as a failure before the men had grasped the importance of the matters they were met to discuss. At last the chairman got up and said, pointing to me, : " Look here, William, could you not say a word if you try, boy ? " I rose in fear and trembling. But I had been very much struck with the line which Lewis Morgan had taken — the necessity of introducing the principle of arbitration in the settlement of labour disputes. They told me afterwards that my speech was a great success, and fairly carried the meeting away with it. I spoke of the evil of retaliation and the dangers, as well as the sweetness, of revenge. The old chairman was delighted, and so was Lewis Morgan. He told me that I must get into harness at once, and begin the organisation of the bituminous coal district. I kept

on my work in the mine, but all my spare time I devoted to
organising and speaking.'[9]

His efforts seem to have been highly successful, for before the
end of 1871 a lodge of the Amalgamated Association of Miners
had been set up at Waunarlwydd, of which Mabon was elected
secretary. Thus at the age of twenty-nine he embarked upon
a career of over forty years as a miners' leader.

It is remarkable that Mabon, who had taken no interest in
trade unionism prior to Lewis Morgan's visit, should have been
elected lodge secretary so soon after joining the movement.
Even allowing for the fact that the Amalgamated Association of
Miners was a new organisation in the area and the first of its
kind, it seems almost incredible that he should have been
chosen in preference to older men. His ability as a speaker,
coupled with his personal popularity, must have stood him in
good stead, and his efforts to win members were no doubt
appreciated by the union's leaders. But the most plausible
reason for his election is that his powers of leadership had
already been demonstrated. Mabon certainly played a
prominent part in a strike which occurred at the Caercynydd
pit during 1871, both as organiser and negotiator. It would
seem likely that the stoppage took place at the time when
Mabon and others were organising the men, and that it was
his conduct during the strike that led to his election.

In the months that followed, Mabon threw all his energies
into building up trade unionism in west Glamorgan and east
Carmarthenshire. The circumstances must have been parti-
cularly favourable, for his efforts bore fruit almost immediately.
Sometime in the spring of 1872 Lewis Morgan again visited the
area, and the Loughor District of the union was formed at a
meeting in the Athenaeum at Llanelly. Mabon was elected
District treasurer, one John Howells of Loughor being chosen
president. So far as can be ascertained this was the first District
of the organisation to be set up in west Wales.

Thus within a matter of months Mabon's eloquence and
organising ability brought him rapid promotion within the
union. To some extent his success was perhaps due to the fact
that he was one of the few leaders who could speak fluently in

Welsh. But his oratory was no less effective in English. In April, 1872, he represented the Loughor District at a national conference of the organisation, and his first speech in English, which was delivered on this occasion, was so successful that he was elected to the National Executive Committee.

It must be remembered that trade unionism had not yet been accepted by the colliery owners, who still regarded union officials as paid agitators. To persist in such activities often meant victimisation, and Mabon's election to the Executive eventually led to his dismissal. The Executive met monthly at Manchester, and his frequent absences were soon noticed by the colliery manager. As a result he was prevented from working at the coalface, and forced to accept the less well paid job of tram-man. A lightning strike lasting four days forced his reinstatement on this occasion, but he was expressly forbidden to leave work in future without the manager's permission. Soon afterwards, however, another meeting of the Executive was called, and as the manager was away from home Mabon again left work without permission. The management replied with an ultimatum that he must either leave the pit or resign his seat on the Executive, and Mabon, having refused to give up union duties, worked his last shift as a collier in December 1872.

With a large family to support Mabon's position was desperate, since no other company could be expected to employ a man branded as a union agitator. But at this critical time he reaped the benefit of all the effort expended in recruiting members to the Loughor District. The District was now sufficiently large to need the services of a paid agent, and Mabon was elected by fifteen of the seventeen lodges.[10]

His gift of Welsh oratory, coupled with the prestige lent by his position as a salaried miners' agent, inevitably made Mabon an important figure in a wider field than he had hitherto known. A strike of the South Wales ironworkers early in 1873 gave him an opportunity to win a reputation throughout the coalfield. He appeared in the Rhondda for the first time later in the same year, advocating conciliation as a better method than the strike of settling industrial problems.[11] His services were sought as conciliator in local disputes, and at Cwm-twrch he had the satisfaction of acting as co-arbitrator with the manager who had dismissed him for his union activities. But despite the many claims upon his time he continued to increase the strength of the Loughor District, and had won no less than eight thousand members to the cause of unionism there by the end of 1874.

While Mabon's rise from collier to miners' agent was impressive if only for its amazing rapidity, it must be admitted that he did not achieve unrivalled prominence until the miners' strike of 1875. Before that date he was but one of many similar apostles of unionism working to organise the workmen, whereas the close of 1876 found him in solitary eminence amid the ruins of the union. The details of this strike need not concern us, but it is necessary to explain how it brought about the collapse of the Amalgamated Association of Miners and, indirectly, the ascendancy of Mabon.

The union had already conducted two important strikes in 1871 and 1873. Both had led to an increase in membership, as often happens during a stoppage, but they had shown clearly that the organisation's funds were insufficient to afford any real strength in a dispute. Moreover, even its membership had fallen during 1874, mainly because financial weakness had forced the Executive to accept several wage reductions rather than risk a stoppage. Since the Amalgamated Association of Miners had been set up solely to deal with the question of wages this had proved a damaging blow to its prestige. Thus the organisation was both numerically and financially weak when the strike began on 1 January, 1875. The stoppage, which lasted five months, completed the destruction of the union. Its funds were exhausted, and it was dissolved during the following summer.

It was during this strike that Mabon first emerged as an influential leader with sharply defined principles and opinions on industrial matters. He not only took his place in the forefront of the movement, but also adopted an independent policy which on occasions clashed with that pursued by Thomas Halliday, the English president of the organisation. Opposition to the established leaders in trade unionism, as in other fields, is often the royal road to popularity, and so it seems to have proved for Mabon.

During the strikes of 1871 and 1873 Halliday had shown a strong sense of responsibility, not hesitating to oppose unwise or dishonourable policies even if they found favour with the rank and file. In addition, he had been extremely sensitive to public opinion, and opposed to violation of contractual agreements, while advocating settlement by conciliation or arbitration. It will be noticed that these views were in later years also characteristic of Mabon, who was no doubt deeply influenced by Halliday's example. But Halliday was less cautious than Mabon, and not so unwilling to use the strike weapon. He was an able, enthusiastic leader who believed that there could be no compromise on a matter of principle. Mabon, on the other hand, was appalled by the hardships suffered by strikers and their families during the stoppage of 1875, and as the months passed he found himself in opposition to Halliday. The sight of miners' children dependent upon public charity and soup kitchens led him to urge acceptance of any reasonable terms. Like Halliday, he at first favoured arbitration, but as the strike continued he showed himself willing to go further in meeting the owners. As he expressed it :

> ' In my opinion it is essential to the creation, maintenance and fostering of that good feeling which should exist between employer and workman — that each should realise their position, — that each should realise that they have equitable rights — and that they should meet together to discuss them. I am perfectly convinced that the only salvation for capital and labour is whole-hearted co-operation between the two sides in forming boards of conciliation and arbitration throughout the country, which would bring peace and prosperity to the industry, without encroaching upon the freedom of either side.'[12]

His solution, which was settlement by conciliation or by arbitration, undoubtedly won considerable support. The Rhondda and Aberdare miners, for example, resolved in April that the strike should be settled by a small committee of owners and men, with an umpire available in case of disagreement. But this was not the policy advocated by Halliday, as Mabon himself makes clear in his account of the stoppage :

' A mass meeting was held at the Drill Hall, Merthyr. (Halliday) was in favour of continuing the struggle, but I made a speech recommending arbitration, which found favour with the delegates. Matters dragged on until the middle of May. Then another meeting was held at Aberdare, when Halliday again advocated a fighting policy. But all through his speech I fancied I could detect a feeling that the dispute would have to be settled by conciliation. I followed him and again strongly advocated that policy — and soon after negotiations were opened with the employers'.[13]

Mabon's views on the strike of 1875 have been considered in some detail because they reflect the principles which underlay his policy throughout his career. It is clear from the quotations given above, for example, that he regarded goodwill and co-operation between workmen and master as indispensable to the prosperity of the industry. Differences should be discussed in a friendly and conciliatory manner, and, if agreement proved impossible, they could be settled by an umpire rather than by industrial warfare. Though the ends of capital and labour seemed diametrically opposed, Mabon believed that since both depended upon the well-being of the same industry there was an underlying identity of interest. Provided both sides approached the question of industrial relations in a friendly spirit and let reason and justice prevail, he believed that the strike would become an obsolete weapon. How far his faith in conciliation was misplaced emerged only during the years that followed.

II

UNIONS AND SLIDING SCALES

THE strike of 1875 provided Mabon not only with a policy but also with a mechanism that enabled him to implement it. The stoppage had been partly a protest against the coal-owner's ability to enforce changes in wages without consulting or giving any explanation to the men. As Mabon observed, the strike was ' not in reality a strike for money but for a principle, namely the right of the workman to have a voice in the sale of his labour'.[1] Neither the men nor their leaders were willing to leave miners' wages completely at the arbitrary discretion of the employers. For that reason they accepted as part of the terms of settlement the establishment of a sliding scale.

The underlying principle of the sliding scale was that wage rates rose or fell in accordance with changes in the average selling price of coal. A certain wage rate was first selected to act as a bench mark or standard. This rate was paid when the average selling price of coal reached a stipulated level, known as the equivalent selling price. When coal prices rose above this level by a predetermined amount, the workmen's wage rates were increased by an agreed percentage. The average selling price of coal was computed from the results of audits taken at regular intervals, and limits were set above and below which changes in coal prices were to have no effect upon wage rates. Thus under the sliding scale agreement of 1875 steam coal miners, for example, were to receive the wage rates paid in 1869 plus 5 per cent when the average selling price of steam-coal reached 12s. per ton. For every rise of 1s. per ton in the selling price of coal above this level, their wage rates were to be increased by $7\frac{1}{2}$ per cent. Audits to determine the average selling price were to be held every six months. If the result was found to be higher than 21s. per ton or less than 12s. per ton, however, the wage rate was to remain unchanged. With each

13

fall of 1s. per ton in the average selling price, of course, the wage
rate was to be reduced by 7½ per cent.

The sliding scale was first proposed by the coalowners, who
were weary of the recurrent strikes arising from wage disputes.
But Mabon seized upon the idea, and soon became one of its
most ardent supporters. It involved no new principle, since
both sides accepted that market conditions, or rather the selling
price of coal, should govern wages. In the past, when coal
prices were high the men had usually forced the employers to
pay higher wages by the threat of a strike, which would have
reduced output and profits. During times of depression, on the
other hand, the owners had generally been able to reduce
wages simply because they could not afford to maintain the
existing rates. The sliding scale was therefore a novelty only in
so far as it would remove the friction which had previously
attended changes in wages, and make strikes or lock-outs
unnecessary.

This was the great advantage of a sliding scale which Mabon
chose to stress. He apparently failed to see its major weakness,
namely that it incited employers to underselling and overproduction, since no matter how greatly coal prices fell, profits
would be maintained by the proportionate fall in wages. The
first agreement defined a minimum wage rate, so that this
defect did not become obvious. But in subsequent years miners'
wages were reduced to subsistence level as a consequence of
the existence of a sliding scale. Theoretically, wages rose very
greatly when prices were high, but in practice times when prices
were low were far more numerous than boom years. In addition, the periods of high prices often lasted only a few months.
Since the audits to discover the average selling price from
which the wage rate was calculated were relatively infrequent,
the boom often passed before wages had risen. Moreover, under
the first agreement the miners received no advance until coal
prices rose by a full 1s., so that the employers alone benefited
from any smaller increase. Only in later agreements was it
conceded that the wage rate should be slightly increased for
even small rises in the price of coal. Further, the use of the
average of prices for the entire coalfield to determine the wage

rate was itself disadvantageous to the men. Long term contracts were often made for large amounts of coal. If these were
made at high prices they could make the average selling price,
and therefore wages, artificially high even if the industry was
depressed. But if they were made at low prices, as was more
frequently the case, they could keep the average price, and the
wage rate, unnaturally low during a boom. It should also be
noted that in the last resort the miners' share in the profits of
the industry depended upon the size of the percentage increase
in the wage rate granted for each rise in coal prices. Under the
agreement of 1875 miners' wage rates were advanced by
$7\frac{1}{2}$ per cent for every 1s. increase in the selling price of coal.
In later years many came to feel that this was not a sufficiently
high percentage to give them their fair share of the industry's
profits.

Mabon may perhaps be excused for failing to foresee the
defects of the sliding scale principle with all its intricacies.
In any case, his main argument in its favour was primarily non-
economic. He hailed its adoption as a promise that there should
be no more strife in the coalfield, and clearly envisaged an era
of peace and justice. The miners presumably shared his belief.
When they elected their representatives on the sliding scale
committee in July 1875 he led the poll with 24,227 votes, and
thus became chairman of the workers' side, a position which
he retained until the sliding scale system was abandoned.[2] In
this committee he found that opportunity for owners and men
to discuss their differences peaceably from which he expected
so much. There, also, he found full scope for his skill as a
negotiator. Although he always had to negotiate from weakness, since the miners lacked an effective organisation until the
end of the century, through his consummate ability he preserved
peace in the coalfield for nearly a generation and, as we shall
see, gained many victories.

But all this lay in the future in 1875, and however much
Mabon's attitude towards the sliding scale principle was tinged
with idealism, he realised that the actual terms of the agreement
might be unfavourable to the men unless the negotiators were
backed by an organised body of workers. For this reason he set

out to rebuild trade unionism in the district. The failure of the
Amalgamated Association of Miners had left the men dispirited,
but there seemed some hope that a purely local organisation
confined to South Wales might win support. Many miners had
objected to the policy of centralisation followed by Halliday's
union, and many more had voiced a demand that dues collected
in South Wales should be retained in the district under the
control of the branches. Even those who saw the value of co-
operation with miners in other coalfields preferred affiliation
to the Miners' National Union. Thus it seemed a good
opportunity to establish what a majority of the men had long
desired, namely, as one miner put it, ' a Welsh union with
Welsh officials, a Welsh treasury and in fact entirely Welsh,
yet retaining a connection with the major union ' (the Miners'
National Union).[3]

Mabon was one of the strongest advocates of an autonomous
union. Even while associated with Halliday's union he had
supported the establishment of a separate central fund in South
Wales, and had taken part in an attempt to revise the organisation's constitution to allow the branches greater independence.
It has even been said that ' the English leaders were the pre-
dominating partners in the Amalgamated Society (sic) of
Miners, and Mabon, convinced that the affiliation of the
English and Welsh Unions was a hindrance, advocated the
severence of the tie.'[4] His arguments against joining the
Miners' Federation twenty years later suggest that his support
for an independent union in South Wales was not based on
nationalism, but on sound economic reasoning. Both the conditions and markets of the coalfield differed from those of other
areas, and he believed that the miners' interests would be best
served by a union limited to South Wales. He was not opposed
to a loose connection with other mining districts, but he
undoubtedly felt that South Wales should always be able, in the
last resort, to go its own way.

Mabon's first plan for reorganising the miners was to
persuade them to rejoin their local lodges. He toured the coalfield, speaking at Llanelly, Ebbw Vale, Tredegar and elsewhere, but met with no success. Nothing could be saved from

the wreckage, and an entirely fresh start had to be made in rebuilding unionism. As an interim measure, a conference held in August decided that the few surviving lodges or Districts should join the Miners' National Union individually, until a constitution could be drafted for a union embracing the entire coalfield. Unfortunately this decision dissolved the last tie between those trade unionists who had preserved some form of organisation. In view of the constitution of the Miners' National Union, it meant that unionism in South Wales would at best be confined to a number of small, independent Districts with limited financial resources. At worst, this policy of piecemeal affiliation laid the way open for further division and disintegration.

The result was disastrous, for non-unionism continued to spread. Even Mabon's oratory could not stem the tide. As he put it, ' We speak to them of unionism and they regard us as hot-heads and agitators, who have a vested interest in its maintenance — and even those who are still union members, through indifference and lethargy and disagreement as to which type of union is best, are irresolute.'[5] The only remaining hope was that the union of South Wales miners mooted in August would prove more popular. A constitution was hastily accepted by a conference on 18 October, and Mabon again toured the district in an attempt to win recruits. But the time for uniting the workmen of the coalfield in one organisation was past. Between August and October the hard core of unionists in Glamorgan and Monmouthshire had splintered into twenty-four preposterously small ' Districts', all separately affiliated to the Miners' National Union and jealous of their independence. The conference of the union in April 1876 which elected Mabon president heard only reports of apathy, indifference and hostility. Total membership cannot have been more than 4000 at this time, and by September 1876 even Mabon had to admit that the great majority of the men were ' outside the societies formed for the defence of labour.'[6]

By this time the coal industry was experiencing a depression, and since the wage rate was now beyond their control the employers sought to reduce labour costs by indirect methods.

For example, allowances or bonuses paid to colliers for work other than hewing coal were abolished, and various other practices were adopted which the men felt to be unjust. This attack on time-honoured customs might well have convinced the miners that a trade union was essential, and on this assumption Mabon made yet another attempt to form an organisation. A conference held on 6 November agreed to reform the existing union and sever all connection with the Miners' National Union, probably in the hope that this would force the small 'Districts' which still remained to unite and sacrifice their independence. But unfortunately a later meeting refused to sanction the merger of all these ' Districts ' into one administrative unit, so that the constitution of the new union did nothing to curb their autonomy. Although Mabon was pessimistic about its future from the first, he did all in his power to make it a success. But by the end of 1876 he was the only miners' agent still active in the coalfield, the others having been forced to find other employment by the total collapse of unionism in their Districts. A final effort was made in August 1877 to revive the long-defunct Amalgamated Association of Miners, on the basis of a low rate of contribution, most of which was to be held in the lodges, presumably as a concession to the desire of the Districts to be autonomous. Halliday consented to act as president, Mabon being elected secretary, but by early September only some seven hundred men had joined, and the union ceased to exist. Except for Merthyr and parts of Monmouthshire, where the Miners' National Union retained some adherents, the cause of unionism was dead.

It is not difficult to find reasons for the failure of trade unionism in South Wales. The destruction of the Amalgamated Association of Miners had left the men dispirited and disillusioned, while some miners could not afford to pay union dues out of their small wages. Under the Miners' National Union the hard core of unionists had become disunited, and the absence of a central authority had fostered indiscriminate splintering and a spirit of particularism in the Districts. This was inevitable to some extent, because the mining valleys were isolated from each other by geographical barriers. But, in addition, the colliers did not all work under the same conditions or serve the same markets, since some were employed by ironworks and others by coalowners, while some mined house coal and the remainder produced steam coal for export. But most important of all, the working of the first sliding scale agreement also undermined the attempts to revive trade unionism.

Since it had been advocated, negotiated and administered by Mabon and the other leaders, the sliding scale was closely identified with the union in the miners' minds. There had been discontent with the actual terms of the agreement, but this was insignificant compared with the outcry that arose when the first audit was announced in February 1876. Coal prices were so low that the men were only entitled to the minimum wage rate. This meant that the miners' wage rates were reduced, and as the award was retroactive any excess pay received since 1st January had to be refunded. The realisation that the minimum wage clause avoided any further reduction prevented the men from abandoning the sliding scale, but the unfavourable agreement reflected discredit on the union and weakened its appeal. Then again, the adoption of a sliding scale removed the main justification for trade unionism by making collective bargaining unnecessary. In practice, the workman who paid his sliding scale levy of a penny per month was no worse off than the miner who paid seven or twelve times as much to his union branch.

But in the last resort the main reason for the failure of trade unionism in South Wales was that the men were not prepared for any form of organisation which embraced the whole area. The Amalgamated Association of Miners had contrived to unite the entire district almost overnight, but it was an unnatural success since it was not based on any tradition of organisation. When that union collapsed the District associations came into their own, for the colliers were still in the first stage of union development and not ready for a county or regional organisation.

Mabon had been prominent in each attempt to revive unionism. He undoubtedly believed that *Mewn undeb mae*

nerth (In union there is strength), and that organisation was
essential if the interests of the workmen were to be safeguarded.
His original aim was clearly the establishment of a strong
Welsh union, allied with similar associations already in existence elsewhere. But by the close of 1877 he had realised that
the miners were not yet prepared for such developments. For
the future he adopted as his objective the fostering of District
unions, which would eventually give way to county or regional
associations and, in time, perhaps become part of a national
organisation. In other words, he abandoned the attempt to
force the establishment of a South Wales union as hopeless,
and set to work to encourage a more natural and gradual
development. From this period dates the real foundation of
mining unionism in the South Wales coalfield.

For Mabon the failure of his attempt to create a regional
organisation was a personal misfortune. The Loughor District
could no longer support a miners' agent, and in February 1877
he removed with his family to the Rhondda, where the men
were still willing to employ a paid representative. He spoke so
convincingly to a mass meeting at Tonypandy on 9 April that
a majority of those present voted to revive unionism in the
valley.[7] Mabon stressed that an organisation was needed not
as a weapon of offence but as a shield, and a conference held
later at Llwynypia decided to form the Cambrian Miners'
Association. At the same time a resolution was also passed
expressing the wholehearted desire of the miners ' that our
agent, Mr. William Abraham, should remain with us.'[8]

The Cambrian Miners' Association was the first of the purely
local organisations that remained typical of mining unionism
in South Wales until 1898. Its activities were confined to the
Rhondda Valley, and its main object was to facilitate co-
operation between employers and workmen. In practice, it was
little more than a machinery for collecting sufficient money to
support Mabon as miners' agent, and the settlement of any
dispute was left entirely in his hands. Owing to its financial
weakness and Mabon's personal views on industrial relations,
the union never adopted an aggressive policy. Since all
problems were resolved by negotiation it neither needed, nor

possessed, a rigid administrative structure. A council was elected to assist Mabon, and a meeting of delegates from all parts of the valley was held monthly, but there were no lodges or branches. Contributions of 1½d, and later 2d, per month were deducted from wages at the colliery offices, the clerks retaining a small percentage for their services. This arrangement made the union officials the servants of two masters, in a sense, but the point is hardly relevant. The organisation was not collecting money to form a fighting fund, and its sole aim was co-operation with the employers. Peaceful agreement was the union's policy, and the system of deductions at least ensured that funds would always be available to pay Mabon for his services as negotiator. Provision was also made for calling levies, but apparently the need never arose.[9] Whatever its defects, the Rhondda miners seem to have been satisfied with this form of organisation, for by 1885 Mabon had recruited some twelve to fourteen thousand members.

The Cambrian Miners' Association was ideally suited to Mabon's purposes, and may be said to reflect his conception of a trade union's functions. It gave him an opportunity to meet the individual employers, to study their characters and estimate what could or could not be won from them. He was empowered to settle grievances in a peaceful manner, which was the only practical manner in view of the men's weak bargaining position. The miners' battles were won not by force but by an appeal to reason and justice, which, owing to Mabon's skill as a negotiator, seldom went unanswered. More-over, the existence of such an organisation was tolerated and even encouraged by the coalowners, since it avoided stoppages. They failed to realise that such an association was in fact laying the foundations of trade unionism such as we know it today.

But while Mabon was putting his principles into practice in the Rhondda, circumstances were conspiring to threaten his policy of co-operation with the employers in the coalfield as a whole. The deepening depression in the coal trade was even menacing the sliding scale agreement, which was the symbol of his conciliatory attitude. As coal prices fell the mine owners had pressed repeatedly for concessions which would enable them to

remain in business. In 1877 they had demanded longer hours
and had sought to negotiate a reduction of the minimum wage
which they were forced to pay. The workmen had rejected
these proposals, but towards the close of 1877 Mabon saw that
the employers were being forced either to dispose of the
minimum wage clause or close their pits. In the prevailing
circumstances the workmen eventually agreed to accept a
reduction of 5 per cent outside the terms of the agreement until
prices revived.

Unfortunately even this concession to the spirit of conciliation by the men had not proved sufficient to solve the coalowners' difficulties. By the autumn of 1878 they found themselves forced to demand either the abolition of the minimum
wage or the abandonment of the sliding scale principle. The
workmen were not prepared to make any further concessions,
and a minority, who felt that they had already gone too far in
conciliating the employers, demanded the resignation of Mabon
and the sliding scale committee. On this occasion even Mabon's
influence could not sway the miners, and the coalowners,
seeing no hope of a peaceful solution, gave notice to terminate
the agreement. Their immediate aim was to free themselves
from the restrictions of the minimum wage clause in order to
enforce a wage reduction of 10 per cent.

Mabon realised that the men's position was hopeless.
Workmen at pits not governed by the agreement were already
working at reduced wages, and the employers in other coalfields
were abrogating their sliding scale agreements or insisting upon
the abolition of the minimum wage clauses. Furthermore, the
men's leaders knew that the industry was in the grip of a severe
depression, and that only a reduction in costs could keep the
pits open. Since the Welsh miners had no effective union, the
coalowners would be able to win further concessions at will.
The men's only safeguard against unlimited reductions was to
preserve the sliding scale, and thus keep wages beyond the
employers' control. To this end Mabon was willing to accept a
10 per cent reduction in wages and even to allow the deletion
of the minimum wage clause from any future agreement. As
he observed : ' The question was how shall we be able to live

after the reduction ? True, but how shall we be able to live after the expiration of the notice, when we will be compelled to accept such reductions as every owner sees fit ?'[10]

These arguments eventually convinced the men that they would have to compromise with the employers, and in March 1879 it was agreed to open negotiations. As a result, a conference held in June reluctantly agreed to accept a wage reduction, but many colliers disregarded this decision and remained idle for from one to four weeks before accepting the lower wages. Others felt that the sliding scale should not be renewed, and advocated the formation of a trade union in the coalfield which could arrange wage rates by normal bargaining processes. The attempt proved abortive, however, and its only result was the establishment of a weak local union in the Aberdare Valley, similar to that existing in the Rhondda. A majority of the workmen appreciated the weakness of their position, and on 17 January, 1880, a new sliding scale agreement was signed.

Its terms are noteworthy because the concept of a minimum wage rate, which had been recognised in 1875, was finally discarded. For the future, miners' wages were to be entirely dependent upon the selling price of coal, with no limitation on their movement. During 1875 Mabon had expressed the view that the workmen should always be paid according to the price reached by the commodity they produced in the open market. But he had also stressed that the workmen should always be able ' to earn enough to keep themselves and their families from poverty and save some amount for a rainy day.'[11] This qualification now ceased to be one of the principles upon which the sliding scale was based. The other terms of the agreement were also perhaps less favourable to the men than to the coalowners, with two notable exceptions. Audits were to be held four times every year, instead of twice yearly as under the last agreement, and wages were to be adjusted as soon as prices changed by 4d. and not by 1s., as had been the case previously. These two modifications made the agreement of 1880 far more sensitive than that of 1875, so that the miners would reap the benefit of even a small increase in prices provided it lasted four

months. This might prove disadvantageous during periods of
falling prices, of course, but the men regarded these clauses as
a victory for their representatives. Nor did they question that
the percentage increase in their wages, granted following each
rise in coal prices, gave them a fair share of the profits of the
industry. So satisfied were the workmen with the new agreement that they requested the owners to deduct their contributions towards its expenses at colliery offices, and even agreed to
press all mine-owners to pay the rates indicated by the various
audits.[12]

The outcome of the negotiations constituted a personal
triumph for Mabon. Faced by a group of employers who were
approaching bankruptcy, and supported by a disorganised
and intransigent body of miners, he had nevertheless contrived
to obtain a settlement. Moreover, by shrewd bargaining and
skilled negotiating he had concluded an agreement in return
for relatively few concessions. A steady rise in wages until
November 1883 served to silence many critics of the terms.
Negotiation of a new and more satisfactory agreement during
1882 passed off without incident, and until the last decade of
the century the history of the sliding scale was one of consistent
modification and improvement.

III

UNPOPULAR POLICIES

In Mabon's view, his main responsibility was that he should, in fact, lead the miners rather than be led by them. His duty was not to avoid criticism or to preserve his popularity, but to put forward constructive policies which would benefit the miners. If the workmen chose to disregard his advice or overrule him he would attempt to persuade them by argument and oratory. But he never feared to recommend unpopular courses of action that he felt to be wise. His was a positive conception of leadership, and he was not content merely to act as a mouthpiece for the workmen's views. But on occasions he inevitably found that the miners were not willing to accept his proposals. Perhaps at no time until 1910 was this more obvious than during the early eighties. While supporting the sliding scale mechanism and encouraging the development of trade unionism, he also advocated other policies which he believed would benefit the miners, but which they refused to adopt.

During 1879 he became a staunch advocate of emigration as a means of preventing further wage reductions. He believed that ' when there is plenty of work and few workmen available wages must be high, but when there is only little work and many workmen wages must be, and generally are, low'.[1] The unsoundness or superficiality of this analysis reflected the state of contemporary economic theory rather than any fault of Mabon's. But since he did not contemplate the destruction of the sliding scale, which tied wages to prices, it is difficult to see how an increase in wages could have come about as a result of the scarcity of labour except indirectly through a reduction of output.

In January 1879 he addressed the Rhondda miners on the question, and created such a deep impression that they endorsed the policy and ordered the publication of his speech.[2] With

the foundation of the Workmen's Emigration Society he became one of its most ardent advocates, organising meetings
which led to the establishment of six branches in the Rhondda.
For an entrance fee of 1s. and a contribution of £5, on which
interest was paid, any member of the society was entitled to
take part in a prize drawing. If selected, he was then sent to
America with £150, which he was to repay in ten years with an
interest payment of the same amount.[3] The Society seems to
have flourished, despite the high fees and exorbitant rate of
interest on loans. But as a method of raising miners' wages it was
clearly doomed to failure.

Perhaps Mabon saw that its success was dependent upon
restriction of output, for in the same year he appeared as a
champion of another and more realistic scheme to raise wages.
Representatives from the various coalfields of Great Britain,
meeting at Barnsley in May 1879, had resolved to demand an
immediate advance of 10 per cent in their wages under threat
of a national strike. Mabon, who had attended, was a member
of the deputation chosen to inform the Miners' National Union
of this decision, and he subsequently spoke in support of it
throughout South Wales.

This attitude is difficult to explain. He apparently believed
that the Welsh miners were justified in using any means to
better their condition, since they received only 3s. 1d. for a ten-
hour day as compared with 5s. 2d. paid for eight hours work in
Northumberland.[4] But he had previously admitted that the
South Wales coalowners could not afford to grant any advance
in wages. The only explanation is that he hoped such a stoppage
would aid the recovery of the industry by driving up the price
of coal.

By this time he had certainly realised the defects of the sliding
scale mechanism when overproduction drove down prices. Pits
sunk in the early seventies were now producing coal and flood-
ing the market, and his solution was to restrict output. His aim,
however, was not to force prices (and therefore wages) up to
an unreasonable level, but merely to combat overproduction,
which had become the curse of the sliding scale mechanism.

The Barnsley Conference had also suggested a general curtailment of working hours as a means of protecting miners' wages. On the advice of the men's sliding scale committee, a conference held in November 1880 resolved to limit the working shift to nine hours, with a view to restricting output. Mabon was perhaps the foremost champion of the nine hours movement. He not only advocated the shorter shift but even warned the men that the scheme would fail if they did ten hours work in nine. Its purpose was to reduce production, and ' if they agreed to sacrifice a tenth of the present output they could undoubtedly expect a two-fold benefit, namely in health and in wages'.[5] His argument was that ' scarcity of the commodity determines the price in every market and country ; create that scarcity by any sound means and the price must inevitably rise.'[6]

The proposal met with some support, for Mabon later thanked the ' friends who have started to carry out the suggestions of the committee.' But June 1881 found him still urging the men to work no more than nine hours, and threatening to publish a list of pits where longer shifts were being worked. When the representatives of the steam-coal miners met in November 1882 to consider output restriction they again resolved to adopt a nine-hour day, but by this time it was clear that the majority of the workmen were opposed to the plan.

On this occasion it was the workmen, and not Mabon, who were in the right. His views had the support of contemporary economic theory. But they were certainly fallacious when applied to an industry which dealt chiefly with foreign markets in which it had no monopoly. It may be said in his favour that the miners' refusal to adopt the scheme was not due to any greater awareness of the economic problems involved. Their decision arose from a realisation that under a piece-work system of payment restriction of output would probably have meant smaller earnings. If scarcity raised the selling price of coal the miner would automatically receive a higher wage rate for each ton that he produced, under the terms of the sliding scale agreement. But this would need to be a substantially higher rate if it was to compensate him for reducing his output by the ten per cent which Mabon suggested. Since the Welsh coal industry was forced to compete with other sources of supply abroad it was even doubtful whether restriction of output could, in fact, raise prices to any great extent. When the supply of Welsh coal on the market was reduced, foreign producers would presumably increase their output to fill the gap, and perhaps even capture markets traditionally supplied by South Wales. The price of Welsh coal might rise temporarily, but in the long run it would be forced down again by the pressure of competition from other sellers.

For Mabon, however, the matter was not yet closed. During December 1882 he attended a conference of delegates from most of the British coalfields which was held at Leeds. Once again, on the grounds that the current overproduction enabled the middleman to exploit both the coalowners and the miners, a decision was taken to restrict coal production. This was to be achieved by adopting either a five-day week or an eight-hour day, and each coalfield was to implement one or other of these schemes in February 1883.

In South Wales, however, the resolutions of the Leeds Conference were completely disregarded. Mabon had attended the meeting on behalf of the Rhondda miners, but no other District had sent a representative. Undoubtedly the majority of the workmen were opposed to restriction of output. The Aberdare colliers, indeed, went so far as to censure their fellow workers in the Rhondda for associating themselves with the movement.[7] A lengthy newspaper controversy developed between the Rhondda and Aberdare miners through the persons of Mabon and David Morgan, their respective leaders, regarding the advantages and disadvantages of output restriction. But eventually even the Rhondda workmen rejected the policy, and resolved not to be represented when the Leeds Conference resumed at Manchester early in 1883.[8]

It was not surprising that even Mabon's powers of persuasion failed on this occasion. David Morgan, for example, condemned output restriction on grounds of principle, pointing out that the colliers would complain bitterly if farmers took similar action to limit the supply of bread. On economic grounds he claimed that dearer coal would find fewer buyers, which would mean either lower wages or unemployment in the industry. But however convincing such arguments may have appeared, the decisive factor for the average collier was that restriction of output meant smaller earnings under a piecework system. Mabon was destined to remain the sole advocate of output limitation in South Wales for some twelve years, until the changed attitude of the employers re-opened the matter.

It was not only in his efforts to safeguard wages, however, that Mabon found himself in opposition to the popular opinion of the miners. Indeed, perhaps the most striking instance occurred with regard to the question of industrial insurance.

None of the trade unions established in South Wales had attempted to arrange or operate sickness or accident schemes. Such matters had, from the first, been left in the hands of either insurance companies or such friendly societies as the Oddfellows or Ivorites. These undoubtedly did good work, but the insurance companies were not popular in the mining areas and many friendly societies were financially unsound. A real need therefore remained for some comprehensive scheme to cater solely for the miners, similar to the Northumberland and Durham miners' Permanent Relief Society, established in 1862.

The South Wales coalowners had proposed an insurance fund ' for the relief and support of those who might be left helpless and penniless by fatal accidents ' as early as 1872. But the matter was not reopened until 1878, when the employers again invited the workmen to co-operate in forming an insurance fund. A miners' conference held in October 1878 agreed to investigate the matter, and appointed a committee of four, which included Mabon, to draft a scheme. Its recommendations as to rates of contribution and benefit proved to be almost identical with those reached by the coalowners' drafting committee. But despite Mabon's wholehearted support for the proposals, which were to a large extent his own work, a miners' conference held in November decided by an overwhelming majority not to co-operate in setting up the fund, and rejected the draft agreed to by its representatives.[9]

Several reasons were advanced in support of this attitude. The main objection — that the rate of contribution proposed was too high in relation to the men's wages,—was perhaps justified. But it was also argued that the coalowners, as the heaviest ratepayers, would benefit when the scheme prevented miners' dependents from becoming a charge on the community: and that no other class in society did anything to prevent members from becoming a burden on the rates. Moreover, it was also hoped that attempts then being made to introduce an Employers' Liability Bill into Parliament would succeed, and make the fund unnecessary.

Late in 1880, however, the employers once again resolved to form a provident fund and, remembering their earlier failure, made no attempt to consult the workmen. The haste with which this Miners' Permanent Provident Society was set up suggests that it was founded mainly so that the coalowners might avoid their responsibilities under the Employers' Liability Act of 1880. This Act granted compensation to workmen injured as a result of their employers' neglect, but did not apply to miners who had ' contracted out ' by joining such an insurance scheme.[10]

Mabon realised the advantages which the scheme conferred upon the workmen. Court cases to secure compensation under the Act would have been expensive, and probably beyond the means of many. The scheme provided for all accidents, including those to which no liability could be attached. Moreover, the coalowners' contribution to the fund would be far greater than any probable liability under the Act, which, in addition, applied only in a few limited cases. And also the scheme was open to men working under sub-contractors, who had no rights under the Act.

It was inevitable that the expert employed by the owners to establish the Society should turn to Mabon in an attempt to win the miners' support.[11] In later years it emerged during a controversy that Mabon was offered the secretaryship of the Society, but declined in order to avoid the suggestion that this support for the organisation had been ' bought'. Nevertheless he became one of its foremost advocates. As early as July 1880 he expressed the view that the forthcoming Liability Act had little to offer the miners. It made no provision for workmen injured as a result of their own carelessness or because of circumstances for which no one was responsible. He foresaw how difficult it would be to prove negligence on the part of the coal-owner or his agent, especially since workmen would be reluctant to testify against their employer. In preference to the unsatisfactory legislation he supported a proposal made by a deputation of mine-owners to Gladstone, namely that a fund from which relief could be given in regard of all accidents should be financed by employers and men.[12]

But the miners as a whole were opposed to the Society, and meetings held throughout the coalfield had decided against supporting it by February 1881. Most of the arguments levelled against the earlier schemes were revived. But the main objection was that to ' contract out ' of the Act's provisions by joining the Society would encourage employers to disregard safety precautions, since they would no longer be liable for damages. At least one miner also feared that if a number of large scale mining disasters occurred, contributions to the fund would be raised, and all members forced to pay them.

With this decision to rely upon the Act and oppose the Society, the miners began preparations to fight for their rights under the Act in the lawcourts. Mabon was forced to withdraw his support for the scheme, and as early as the autumn of 1881 the Cambrian Miners' Association altered its rules to establish a Defence Fund to meet legal expenses. With the aid of this fund the Association successfully contested the case of an Abergorci boy who lost an arm in a colliery accident, but this was the only case fought in South Wales under the Act during 1881.[13] An attempt to form a Defence Fund for the whole coalfield was frustrated by lack of union organisation, and although conferences met and rules were drafted, it never came into existence.[14] As a correspondent to the *Tarian y Gweithiwr* observed, the men had opposed the Miners' Permanent Provident Society but had done nothing to provide an effective alternative. As time passed opposition to the Society weakened, since there was little hope of benefit from the Act without the existence of a Defence Fund. There was no flood of litigation, and the Society gained in strength from year to year until it embraced nearly one-half of the labour force in the coalfield by 1887. It continued to prosper, and by 1912 over £917,373 had been paid out in widows' pensions, funeral allowances, disability pensions and, later, old age pensions.

Mabon's attitude towards the question of industrial insurance underlines an aspect of his character which is especially praiseworthy. He gained nothing from his support of the Miners' Permanent Provident Society or similar projects ; indeed, he continually risked unpopularity in his attempts to persuade the miners to follow policies which he felt to be wise. His reason was undoubtedly the hardship experienced by the miners' families after an accident, whether it brought death or the almost equally crushing blow of disablement. It was chiefly the suffering which it involved for the colliers' dependents that convinced Mabon of the futility of the strike weapon. No doubt it was the memory of the miners' families at the soup-kitchens in 1879 that led him to advocate emigration and output restriction. His concern was always for those who suffered most when there was unemployment, when wages were low, and when the miners stopped work. He always felt responsible for them, and his conscience would let nothing stand in the way of their best interests.

IV

WIDER HORIZONS

IN THE period after 1877 Mabon became a well-known and respected figure in the Rhondda. By 1885 he was a member of the school board and president of the Ystrad Literary and Debating Society, and in 1887 his services to the district were recognised by his appointment as justice of the peace. At the same time his position as vice-chairman of the sliding scale committee, and his pre-eminence as a miners' leader, made his name familiar throughout South Wales. During 1878 he appeared at Cardiff to protest against the introduction of Indian troops into Europe, where ' his unadorned eloquence was so overwhelming that he carried the whole meeting away with him.' In 1880 he was at Swansea, speaking to a conference of tinplate workers at which their trade union was formed. During 1886 he attended the anthracite miners' annual demonstration at Cwmamman, and concluded the proceedings by singing *Hen Wlad fy Nhadau*.

In the course of 1883 he published his first pamphlet, entitled *Political Economy and the Education of the Working Classes*, of which unfortunately no copy seems to have been preserved. But his articles in the *Tarian y Gweithiwr*, the *South Wales Daily News*, and the *Western Mail* alone are sufficient to underline his pre-occupation with industrial matters. Although he frequently dealt with aspects of industry and commerce in other countries, his main interest was the South Wales coalfield. Even his earliest articles show a remarkable insight into its problems. They abound in facts and figures, which are handled with complete confidence despite their complexity, and make it clear that Mabon's knowledge of the industry was at least equal to that of any other expert. This must have been generally realised, for in 1885 Mabon was offered the post of assistant inspector of mines in the district. And it was typical of Mabon that he

33

declined, on the grounds that he would not then be free to represent the miners.

But although he was well known in the coalfield by 1885, it was his entry into Parliament that made him a national figure.

The Franchise Act of 1884 gave voting power to miners everywhere, but nowhere was more political enthusiasm aroused than in the Rhondda, which became a separate electoral division. As early as July 1884 the Cambrian Miners' Association had censured the House of Lords for obstructing the bill, and resolved that the Rhondda was qualified to become a new parliamentary constituency. In view of the pending general election, a delegate conference representative of the entire coalfield decided, during April 1885, that a miners' candidate should enter the contest. But the matter was dropped, and only in the Rhondda, perhaps the one constituency where mining voters predominated, did a candidate come forward with the workmen's support.

The choice inevitably fell upon Mabon, who was adopted as candidate by a mass meeting of miners in opposition to a coal-owner, F. L. Davis, sponsored by the Liberals. The election platforms of both candidates were typically Liberal. The only significant difference was that Davis held the view that the member for any division should represent all his constituents. Mabon, on the other hand, believed that the interests of the miners would be better represented by a collier than by a coal-owner.[1] Indeed, the Liberal 'Three Hundred', which had selected Davis as candidate in preference to Mabon, was widely criticised as being composed of mine-owners and not representative of the workmen. Undoubtedly the appearance of a miners' candidate, and the bitterness which characterised the election campaign, arose because the miners regarded it as an extension of the underlying conflict between employer and employed. Hecklers at Davis' meetings did not attack his Radical programme, but rather the fact that mechanics at his collieries worked a twelve hour day, or that he opposed weekly payment of wages. Reminders of the many philanthropic actions performed by the Davis family were met with cries of ' our money ' and

' profits from the small coal'. And on at least one occasion Davis was compelled to leave a meeting under police protection.[2]

Enthusiasm ran high among the miners, even the children playing their part in supporting Mabon. The ' Mabonites', as they were termed, broke up so many of Davis's meetings that he was eventually forced to adopt the practice of admission by ticket. His supporters had their windows broken, and at one time the *South Wales Daily News* stated that clergymen and tradesmen were being intimidated for supporting the Three Hundred. But it was never suggested that Mabon encouraged such behaviour, and although his candidature amounted to rebellion against the official Liberal organisation, many prominent party members addressed meetings on his behalf. Indeed, there is a tradition that Gladstone himself contributed fifty pounds to Mabon's election expenses, which is not unlikely in view of the friendship which developed between the two men.

The poll revealed a majority of 867 in Mabon's favour, who thus became the first member for the Rhondda, a position which he retained until the Rhondda was divided into two constituencies in 1918. From 1918 until his retirement in 1920 he represented the Rhondda Western division. It is worth noting that Mabon's election expenses and also a living allowance of £160 per annum were raised by public subscription, the Rhondda Liberal and Labour Association being formed in December 1885 to organise the fund. Mabon entered Parliament on 25 January 1886, and delivered his maiden speech, on the subject of Disestablishment, in the following March. His election appears to have healed the division in the local Liberal party, for he was never opposed by a Liberal candidate at any future election. As a result he was returned unopposed on several occasions. Conservative opponents he defeated with ease in 1900 and 1910, his majority in the election of 1900 being the largest in the country. It is significant that even when opposing his industrial policy the Rhondda miners never hesitated to return him as their member.

Mabon was not an outstanding parliamentarian, although his frequent use of the Welsh language in the House attracted

considerable attention. He belonged rather to that small group
of men whose opinions were universally respected and who
were content not to speak when they had nothing to say. But,
as the editor of the *Railway Review* observed, when Mabon
spoke he always had an important contribution to make to the
discussion, and he said it in such a manner that everyone
heard and believed it.[3]

Indeed, indications are not lacking that, given the time and
the inclination, Mabon could have made a highly successful
political career. Gladstone, for example, is said to have offered
him the post of under-secretary at the Home Office, and many
of his speeches were models of oratory. His speech urging
government intervention in the South Wales colliers' strike of
1897 was hailed as brilliant, and of his speech on the Coal
Mines Bill of 1887 it was said that none was more favourably
received. According to one account :

> ' His figures and quotations from the Report of the Royal
> Commission were effectively marshalled ; the delivery was
> deliberate and emphatic, and the speech was listened to with
> marked attention by the Home Secretary and his Under-
> Secretary, who took ample notes of it, and with admiration
> and approval by the Liberals and many of the Conservatives.
> Young Tories were touched by his pathetic but manly appeals
> for the coalminer in his perilous work. One passage, in which
> he described death occasioned by the falling of roofs and sides,
> was delivered with some eloquence, and any other assembly
> than such a Saxon one as the House of Commons would
> have given some more demonstrative expression to its roused
> emotion than their cheers to Mabon's description of the fell
> certainty with which the " Angel of Death snatches his occa-
> sional victim — here today, there tomorrow, without the
> outburst of popular grief or gloom occasioned by a great
> explosion which arouses public attention ". '[4]

Mabon figured prominently in debates on questions relating to
Wales, the Welsh language and the interests of the working
classes. But his main concern was with mining legislation, to
which he contributed much from his knowledge and experience.
The Workmen's Compensation Act, the Employers' Liability
Act and, of course, the Eight Hours Act, owed much to his
eloquence and influence.

His most important parliamentary work, however, was done not on the floor of the House but in connection with various committees and commissions. He was a member, for example, of the Select Committee on mining leases and wages in Devon and Cornwall, which shaped the Stannaries Act in 1887. He was also a member of the Royal Commission on Mining Royalties appointed in 1889, of the Royal Commission on Labour of 1891 and of the Royal Commission on Mines of 1906. In all three he played an important part. With regard to the Commission of 1906, whose findings led to the Mines Regulation Act of 1911, the separate report produced by Mabon, Enoch Edwards and Robert Smillie aroused wide-spread attention. Again, the minority report of the Royal Commission on Labour, regarding the sweated industries, prepared by Mabon, Tom Mann and others, was published as a pamphlet and praised by Sidney Webb. Nor was Mabon unaware of the need for legislation on other matters, for he was associated with the introduction into Parliament of an Eight Hours Bill in 1894 and an Intermediate Education Bill for Wales in 1888.

Mabon's prestige as a member of Parliament was, of course, important outside the House, and as a result he also played a prominent part on various deputations. In connection with the Mines Bill of 1887 alone, for example, he was a member of two such deputations, one from the miners and the other from the employers. In the same year he also visited the Foreign Office to express the workmen's objections to the system of foreign bounties. During 1893 and 1896 he met Gladstone and the secretary of state respectively to advocate the eight-hour day, and in 1905 visited the chancellor of the exchequer to urge the removal of the tax on coal exports. Indeed, he continued to act on deputations even after he had severed his connection with the South Wales miners, although his activities in this direction were mainly concerned with the coal industry.

Despite the fact that Mabon always chose to regard himself as a representative of labour, his political convictions were, with this reservation, those of the Liberal party. It is doubtful

whether he appreciably modified his views even when the
miners compelled him to join the Labour party in 1909. This
did not mean that he refused to act in concert with the other
miners' members of Parliament, such as Burt and Pickard.
Indeed, their frequent meetings to discuss policy led many
persons to speculate as early as 1886 as to whether a parliamentary labour party was being formed. But all these men in
fact held Liberal opinions, and did not consider an independent
policy advisable. In practice these Liberal-Labour, or 'Lib-
Lab ', members accepted the Liberal whip.

This is especially true of Mabon, who, at least during his
early years in Parliament, was prominent in the South Wales
Liberal Federation. He was deeply involved in the political
issues of the day, and frequently spoke throughout the district
in support of the policies and candidates of the Liberal party.
His efforts for the Liberal party were recognised in 1888, when
he was selected to represent South Wales on a deputation
which the party sent to Ireland.[5] At the same time he was also
an active member of the unofficial group formed by the sixteen
Welsh Liberal members of Parliament to discuss matters affecting Wales. And some of his most successful speeches in the
House were delivered in debates upon such questions as
Disestablishment.

Mabon's association with the Liberal party in and out of
Parliament brought him into contact with many of the most
eminent men of his day. He developed a close friendship with
Gladstone, for example, with whom he frequently discussed the
Welsh people and their love of music. They often dined together, and Mrs. Gladstone presented Mabon with a silver leek
to wear on his first Saint David's Day in the House of Commons.
But perhaps of greater interest today is the part played by
Mabon in the careers of notable Welshmen. During his early
years in Parliament he was closely associated with Thomas
Edward Ellis, and travelled to North Wales to support him in
the election of 1886. After his victory at the polls Ellis returned
the favour and appeared in the Rhondda to support Mabon's
candidature. They later worked together on many occasions,
notably in the successful revolt against an attempt by the

Liberal party to force an unpopular candidate upon the electors
of west Glamorgan. Mabon also gave considerable assistance
to David Lloyd George in the campaign which led to his
election in 1890. As early as 1885 Mabon predicted that Lloyd
George would one day be prime minister, and willingly
addressed the electors of Caernarvonshire on his behalf when
asked to do so. Mabon himself has described the events that
followed :

> ' I remember well Mr. Lloyd George's first election, and a
> keen, hard contest it was, as the narrow majority proved.   I
> was invited to his assistance when the crisis was crucial, and
> I readily responded. A. J. Balfour at that period was decidedly
> unsympathetic towards Welsh national aspirations, and in a
> speech he had just then delivered he had dismissed with a
> cynical Latin phrase the Welsh claim of distinct nationality.
> I seized the occasion and composed a satirical poem in Welsh
> with the Latin phrase as a refrain. It added the little extra
> stimulus at the critical stage of the contest to ensure success,
> for the song enjoyed immense popularity among the Caer-
> narvonshire quarrymen and we literally sang the future prime
> minister into parliament'.[6]

From that time forward Mabon and Lloyd George co-operated
in Parliament on many issues, and when the latter became
prime minister it was through Mabon that he appealed to the
miners for their support in the prosecution of the war.

The policy of the South Wales Liberal Federation was more
Liberal than Welsh Nationalist, despite its concern with the
problem of Home Rule in Ireland. The same is true of Mabon.
But it cannot be doubted that he was deeply and sincerely
conscious of the needs and aspirations of Wales. His love of the
traditional culture of Wales, its poetry and its language, found
expression on many occasions both within the House of
Commons and elsewhere. He was especially proud of the Welsh
language, the language which gave full scope for his powers of
oratory, and he never failed to do all in his power to win
recognition for it. It was Mabon, for example, who seconded
the motion that led to the formation of the Society for the
Utilisation of the Welsh Language, which later became the
Cymdeithas yr Iaith Gymraeg.[7] It was also he who pressed for the
inclusion of Welsh in the list of subjects enumerated in the

Education Code during 1887, and repeatedly urged that all
mines inspectors in South Wales should be able to speak the
Welsh language. To make his point more forcibly Mabon
would often confound the House of Commons by speaking in
Welsh. But perhaps never did he use this device with greater
effect than during the debate on Lloyd George's motion
expressing regret at the appointment of non-Welsh speaking
judges in 1892. While stressing the importance of the motion
Mabon suddenly launched into an unbroken flow of Welsh,
at which some members broke into laughter. Mabon continued
until the mirth had subsided, and then calmly informed them
that they had been laughing at the Lord's Prayer.

But Mabon was not only concerned with the survival of the
Welsh language. He was equally interested in the needs of
Wales as a nation. On many occasions he emphasised that he
would ' endeavour to initiate and carry legislative measures
that will meet the just and natural claims of Wales'.[8] Although
he may have expressed himself more strongly than he intended
in the heated atmosphere generated by the question of Irish
Home Rule, his speeches throughout 1887 and 1888 made
many references to the need for Home Rule for Wales and
Scotland. It is not clear what measure of Home Rule Mabon
desired for Wales. During December 1886 he spoke in favour of
a resolution ' that it is imperative that a measure of Home Rule
be granted to Wales.'[9] Apparently he visualised the formation
of a Welsh national executive with power to deal exclusively
with Welsh questions. This was certainly part of the platform
of that candidate for west Glamorgan who was elected after
Mabon and Thomas Edward Ellis had forced the nominee of
the party organisers to withdraw. In view of his ingrained
caution it is not likely that Mabon supported any more
revolutionary scheme. He was, however, convinced that a
Welsh party was needed in the House of Commons to watch
over the interests of Wales.[10] The Liberal members who
represented Welsh constituencies did, in fact, consult together
on questions affecting Wales. But this was the nearest approach
made to the formation of such a party. In practice, Welsh
interests were generally made subservient to other political

considerations by the leaders of the Liberal party.

Mabon's activities in the years that followed his entry into Parliament were many and varied. He would frequently represent the relatives of men killed in colliery accidents at the inquests which followed. Miners prosecuted for breaches of colliery rules would often find him present in court to safeguard their interests. At a demonstration of electrical shot-firing at Ynys-hir in 1887 Mabon himself fired twenty-one shots, and carefully examined both the apparatus and the system of lighting the pit by electricity. Like many self-taught men he was keenly interested in education, and on several occasions opened new schools or presented prizes to students at technical classes. At other times he would give lectures on his experiences in Parliament and other subjects of general interest, and of course he continued to write for the contemporary press. But even so he still found time to devote to the two influences which had played such a large part in his life, namely the chapel and the eisteddfod.

No study of Mabon's life would be complete without some reference to his activities in connection with the eisteddfod, for he became a member of the Gorsedd of Bards at the Brecon National Eisteddfod of 1889. Since his early years at Cwmavon Mabon had taken a keen interest in this aspect of Welsh culture. But as he became better known in the coalfield he played an increasingly prominent part in such functions, not as a competitor, but as adjudicator or master of ceremonies. Even before moving to the Rhondda he had been accustomed to act as adjudicator in local competitions, but after 1877 his attention was also drawn to the National Eisteddfod. By 1887, when it was announced that he was to conduct at the National Eisteddfod in London, he was sufficiently well known to these circles for the *South Wales Daily News* to observe that ' Mabon is expected to take the palm, the other two being, comparatively speaking, untried men in this work'.[11] At this meeting Mabon's ability to dominate large gatherings was strikingly demonstrated. The proceedings were delayed by the absence of the pianist and the audience became restive ; Mabon tried to pacify them by telling a story but even this failed, and it was not until he started to sing that order was restored.[12]

Through the National Eisteddfod Mabon came to meet
many eminent poets and singers. He formed a close friendship,
for example, with Dyfed, who composed the magnificent
epitaph which appears on Mabon's tombstone. At the eisteddfod of 1889 he met the celebrated Adelina Patti, who compli-
mented him upon his fine voice. But he was happiest when
attending the local choral festivals of the miners, which were
often held on Mabon's Day, the monthly holiday which he
inaugurated in the coalfield. They gave him an opportunity to
meet the men whom he led and represented, and of whom he
was always so proud. As he told two members of Parliament
present at an eisteddfod in Ynys-hir, ' These are my men ; the
marks of their labour are on their hands, but if their hands are
hard, they have soft hearts.'[13]

Immediately on his arrival in the Rhondda Mabon became
associated with Nazareth Calvinistic Methodist Chapel, Pentre,
and took an important part in its religious life. Soon after
becoming a member he was made precentor at that chapel, and
also assumed responsibility for the Band of Hope. His connection with Nazareth remained unbroken until his death,
for he worshipped there regularly and contributed generously
towards the financial needs of the chapel, although he did not
become a deacon. His main interest was, of course, the choir,
and while many knew more of the theory of music, Mabon well
understood the meaning of each hymn. It was generally
admitted that the singing was more fervent and inspired when
under his leadership.

During the last decade of the century the vital part played by
religion in his life was shown even more clearly, for Mabon
himself became a lay-preacher. Fortunately a few of his sermons
have been preserved at the National Library of Wales, and
these, together with the recollections of the many persons who
heard him, provide a clear picture of his homely eloquence. It
appears that his sermons, like his speeches and lectures, were
generally delivered extempore. Indeed, at times he would
become so enthusiastic as to lose the thread of his discourse,
until, realising this, he would suddenly stop speaking with
' Now just a minute, where are we ? ' But if his sermons lacked

polish, his eloquence and sincerity more than compensated for the defect. The Rev. Thomas Charles Williams, sometime moderator of the General Assembly of the Presbyterian Church of Wales, spoke highly of Mabon's discourses, as did such celebrated preachers as Dr. P. T. Forsyth and Dr. Campbell Morgan. All three once heard Mabon at Llandrindod Wells, and Dr. Forsyth after thanking him for the service, told his friends ' that sermon did my soul good. We are in danger of being too academic in our presentation of the Gospel — after all, the Gospel never looks better than in plain clothes'. Yet perhaps the best testimony to the effectiveness of Mabon's homespun delivery is to be found in the popularity which he enjoyed as a preacher, since for many years he was welcomed by the worshippers at chapels of all denominations throughout South Wales.

Despite his many activities, however, it must be remembered that Mabon's vocation was that of miners' leader, and most of his time was devoted to that task. To the present generation of miners the speeches which Mabon delivered in his early career would certainly seem strange. When he was present the colliers' meetings often opened with a short prayer, and the atmosphere was more that of an elders' meeting than of a trade union conference. The emphasis of his addresses was as much upon duties as upon rights, for despite his ability as an orator he refused to adopt the methods of the demagogue. His speeches frequently took the form of moral homilies, and while discussing various problems he would often pause to urge the miners to be frugal, sober and diligent. He consistently advocated conciliation as a better means than the strike weapon for settling disputes. Indeed, his repeated reminder that half a loaf was better than no bread, given, of course, in Welsh, became proverbial in the coalfield. Mabon's plea was always for moderation, and for a generation his appeals seldom went unheeded.

It must be remembered that almost until the turn of the century the miners' agent enjoyed a remarkable power over the men he represented. The general feeling was that he was better educated than they were, and that it was foolish to criticise one who was better qualified to form decisions on industrial problems. Indeed, only when the study of economics and politics became widespread did the men's leaders find their authority challenged and their prestige undermined.

Yet Mabon did not owe his supremacy solely to the authority of his position. His personal qualities alone would perhaps have made him pre-eminent. First among these was his refusal to act without caution and forethought. As he put it, ' I decided from the first that whatever happened I would keep my head. When a man loses his head he loses everything'.[14] Even in the most heated discussions he always remained calm, and on many occasions his refusal to be angered served him well in his dealings with both employers and workmen. In addition, however, Mabon was also a keen student of human nature, and knew well the characteristics of the men he led. Years of experience had taught him how to amuse them with a story or capture their imagination with a catch-phrase, how to please or pacify them with a song, and how to drive home his point with a homely simile or parable.

One incident which revealed his knowledge of the miners' temperament occurred when he was addressing the colliers of the Bristol district. He arrived to find the hall empty, although many workmen were gathered near the building, smoking and chatting. Instead of making a direct appeal to them to take their places at the meeting Mabon sat down at a piano which was available, and played a few popular tunes. Soon a dozen men had come in to listen, and he began to sing in his rich tenor voice, accompanied by these miners. The hall quickly filled, so that ' when the speaking commenced he was able to address as big a gathering as had assembled in Bristol for some time.'[15]

Mabon also used similar methods on many occasions during his career to silence hecklers or quell disorder at miners' meetings. Indeed, there was some justification for the remark once made by one of Mabon's brothers that ' our Bill was always fond of singing. He has now sung himself into the position of miners' leader'. If for any reason he was unable to make himself heard, owing to interruptions or cat-calls, he rarely appealed for order. More frequently he would begin to sing some well-known hymn, and gradually the uproar would cease as the colliers joined him, each taking his part until the unruly assembly was transformed into a great choir. Then, when the hymn was over, Mabon would begin to speak in the silence that followed, and under the spell of his oratory his critics would be powerless.

Even Mabon's personal bearing was impressive and commanded respect. He was of only medium height, but well-built, and a long black beard added to his imposing appearance. With middle-age his weight increased, so that Keir Hardie described him in 1888 as being ' five feet by four feet, correct measurement, so that he is not as broad as he is long, though I should say he soon will be'.[16] But this undoubtedly enhanced rather than detracted from the impressiveness of his demeanour.

Perhaps most important of all in commanding respect, however, was the obvious sincerity with which Mabon advocated the policies in which he believed. If his actions were criticised he never hesitated to go before the miners to justify them. When the colliers embarked upon some course of which he disapproved, he, in turn, did not fail to tell them that they were in the wrong, even if it meant admitting that the employers were right. During the nineties Mabon's refusal to compromise with his conscience brought him into considerable personal danger as well as unpopularity. While the Hauliers' Strike of 1893 was in progress, for example, his efforts to address a hostile meeting ended in failure, and a threatening mob of hauliers followed him to his home. He was only able to escape owing to the courage of one David Hughes, who was well-known as a skilful boxer and came forward to challenge the best man among them. Again, during the strike of 1898 he received several letters threatening his life for being ' false to the Labour cause', but Mabon characteristically refused to be ' deterred from doing his duty by any such intimidation'.[17]

It must also be admitted that Mabon's attitude towards the employers and his way of dealing with them would seem strange today. The virtual absence of union organisation naturally meant that he was always compelled to negotiate with the coal-owners from a weak position. But it was in any case his firm conviction that conciliation was the best means of resolving disagreements. He was perhaps as fully conscious of the rights of the employers as of those of the men. He met them in a friendly manner with an appeal to their sense of justice, and was careful never to provoke or threaten them. This did not mean that he sought peace at any price, for he clung tenaciously to what he regarded as being the miners' just and reasonable demands. But in most cases his solution to a dispute was a compromise acceptable to both parties.

Perhaps surprisingly, his methods appear to have proved fairly successful, which was no doubt largely due to his skill as a negotiator and the force of his personality. Yet today it is difficult to conceive of a dispute being settled by the means often employed by Mabon. On one occasion, for example, he met a young coalowner to consider a dispute which had arisen at his collieries, but after saying a short prayer he made no attempt to discuss the matter. Mabon merely told the employer that he was a close friend of his father, expressed the hope that they, too, would be good friends, and left to tell the miners that the question was settled. Even when convinced of the justice of some demand made by the men Mabon would maintain his moderate attitude. If he desired an increase of 2d. in the cutting price at some pit, he would first ask an increase of half that amount and request the remainder some time in the future. It will be noticed, however, that such methods required a man of outstanding ability to make them effective. In addition, they could only succeed so long as he had the full confidence of the miners and, most important of all, the conscious or unconscious co-operation of the employers.

Although his policies were frequently attacked, it is safe to say that until 1910 Mabon remained the unquestioned leader of the South Wales miners. On the whole he enjoyed the full confidence of the workmen, despite short periods of unpopularity. At the turn of the century he was the most prominent figure in the mining world of South Wales, and the extent of his popularity may be gauged by the fact that his name printed on a packet of tobacco or on a bottle of sauce was sufficient to ensure the success of the product.

V

THE ATTACK UPON THE SLIDING SCALE

BETWEEN 1885 and 1887 a recession in the coal industry and the associated fall in coal prices led to an unbroken series of wage reductions. As Mabon observed :

> ' The bulk of colliery labour in this district is now reduced in wages within 5 per cent of what it was in the years 1877 and 1879 — the years of relief committees and soup kitchens. In other words, it will be at the same point as it was in 1880 — with this marked difference, that the work at the collieries was more regular in 1880 than it is at the end of 1886, in consequence of which disputes and indirect encroachments upon the rates of wages are more now than then'.[1]

As a result an attempt was made to revise the sliding scale agreement with a view to improving wages, and notice of termination was served during 1887.

There was little antagonism to the sliding scale principle, but only to the current terms. Indeed, when the employers refused to revise the agreement the workmen withdrew their notice, rather than risk losing the sliding scale principle. By exploiting this situation the employers were even able to win a guarantee that notice would not be served again for at least two years. But there was manifest disappointment among the men at their failure to gain a more favourable settlement, especially the inclusion of a minimum wage clause. Recent experience had convinced them that a sliding scale without such a clause could mean starvation. A minority, indeed, perhaps realised that by tying wages to prices a sliding scale gave the employers an incentive to overproduction. Moreover, some miners clearly felt that the sliding scale was giving them too small a share in profits. Undoubtedly criticism of the sliding scale principle was becoming more serious and intelligent, so that the discussions of 1887 reflected a deep-seated discontent.

Mabon, as usual, championed the sliding scale, and his influence was probably decisive in persuading the men to accept the agreement. His main argument was that until a better method of wage regulation was practicable it was futile to destroy the sliding scale. While no bridge existed across the river it was senseless to abandon the plank which had hitherto served its purpose.[2] It gave steadiness to trade and wages, and the agreement could only be objectionable if it prevented the men from obtaining a fair share of the profits. He admitted that it was his ' honest conviction that the men do not receive the full percentage that they ought'.[3] But, apart from this, the new agreement was as good as any in the Kingdom when prices rose above 9s. 2d. per ton.

The clearest indication of the men's discontent with their wages, however, was an attempt made to revive trade unionism during the negotiations. One section of the colliery workmen had already contrived to organise themselves, namely the enginemen and stokers. After two abortive attempts in 1883 and 1884 they had finally established a general union during 1885. The task had been relatively easy, since they were few in numbers and at least semi-skilled. Moreover, low wages and long working hours provided a strong incentive towards united action.

But their success encouraged the men's leaders to renew their efforts to organise the general body of the miners.

A conference held in October 1887 to discuss the sliding scale appointed a committee, which included Mabon, to draft a constitution for a general union. Its work was accepted by a further conference in January 1888, and as a result the South Wales and Monmouthshire Colliery Workmen's Federation came into being.[4] The organisation, which was to be administered by a committee elected annually, embraced the members of all existing local or District unions, who were to pay ¼d. monthly to meet expenses. In effect it was merely a loose confederation of the existing associations, and mainly intended to further parliamentary agitation. The executive committee was empowered to deal with disputes referred to it by the Districts, and to call levies in certain circumstances. But, although it represented a step forward, the new union was no stronger than its constituent parts, the Districts, and had no real influence over their actions.

Nevertheless Mabon, who was of course elected president of the organisation, apparently believed that it would prove effective. The first issue to arise concerned the adoption of an eight hour working day, a policy which the union included among its objectives. In October 1887 Mabon had proposed to an international miners' conference at Edinburgh ' that eight hours be made the maximum working day for miners underground'. But a committee set up to consider the matter, of which he was a member, turned the issue into one of output restriction.[5] It recommended an eight hour day, but went further than Mabon had envisaged by advising a stoppage on one day in each week, a strike of seven days to reduce stocks, and agitation for a general increase of 10 per cent in wages. Obviously Mabon could not support this policy, since wage rates in South Wales were tied to the sliding scale. He therefore replied to a subsequent conference on behalf of the South Wales miners that his district would only press for the eight hour day.

The defection of South Wales proved the death blow of the scheme. Although some miners in the Caerphilly area and those employed by the Ocean Company decided to adopt the weekly holiday, the majority undoubtedly opposed the Edinburgh plan. Their aim was a statutory eight hour day which would benefit their health and lead to a fuller life, not merely restrict output and reduce earnings.

But in one direction the discussion of this matter bore fruit. In June 1888 a conference of the union resolved, on the advice of the executive committee, to declare the first Monday in each month a holiday throughout the coalfield. This holiday, which came to be known as Mabon's Day, was undoubtedly a great boon to the workmen. It made life more pleasant for the miner who, in the winter months, rarely saw daylight except on Sunday, and gave him time for the eisteddfod, for sports and for social intercourse. Moreover, it facilitated the conduct of union affairs by ensuring that every workman was free to attend meetings at least once in each month. Indeed, it is not surprising that this holiday is remembered even today as one of Mabon's outstanding achievements. But as a means of restricting output or increasing employment it was, of course, a failure.

Perhaps encouraged by its success in introducing this holiday, the union next turned its attention to the question of wages. In view of the improvement in coal prices during 1888 the central coalfields of England had initiated a successful campaign for an increase of 10 per cent in wages. This forward policy found considerable support among the South Wales miners who, although bound by the sliding scale agreement, felt that it was time to press for a bonus advance outside its terms. This attitude was significant, since in theory the men had only to bide their time for the sliding scale to raise their wages. There was clearly discontent with the working of the current agreement. Many workmen believed that it did not give them a fair share of the profits of the industry, for example, and that it was too insensitive to award them the benefits of a brief increase in prices.

A conference of the union in November 1888 therefore resolved to demand a bonus increase of 10 per cent. Since coal prices were improving the employers proved willing to grant an advance of half that amount, and to revise the agreement so as to make it more sensitive. But in return they sought the abolition of Mabon's Day, which was apparently costing the Powell-Duffryn Company £20,000 per annum because of absenteeism on the following day. The miners were in no mood to trifle, however, and in February 1889 they rejected these proposals, demanded an increase of 12½ per cent, and served notice to terminate the agreement. A stoppage was only averted by the owners' willingness to grant a 10 per cent wage increase, and the negotiation of a new agreement began under very strained conditions.

The men's demands were far reaching. They included a raising of the standard, which meant an increase in the wage rate unless the equivalent selling price was also raised ; a minimum wage clause ; modifications to make the scale more sensitive ; a higher percentage increase in the wage rate for each advance in coal prices ; an eight hour day ; exclusion of long contracts from the audits ; and payment for any small coal produced, on the grounds that industrial uses had now been found which made it valuable.[6] Nearly all were concerned with wages and the defects of the sliding scale which apparently worked to the men's disadvantage. The demands were almost certainly more than the employers could afford to concede, but the miners flatly refused to give their representative a free hand to negotiate, showing that they would not compromise. In August the employers were forced to grant a further wage increase of 5 per cent pending a settlement. Finally, however, the coalowners rejected the men's demands in their entirety during December 1889, and it appeared probable that the sliding scale would cease to exist.

This was all the more likely since the elements who were discontented with the sliding scale now had a rallying point, namely the Miners' Federation of Great Britain. This organisation, which comprised those English coalfields that had initiated a campaign for higher wages, was set up by a conference held at Newport in October 1889. Mabon had attended on behalf of South Wales but withdrew, along with the Durham miners' representatives, when a resolution was passed condemning the sliding scale principle.[7] The new union advocated the establishment of conciliation boards with provision for a minimum wage rate, and favoured an aggressive policy. Thus all who opposed the sliding scale principle were provided with an alternative policy, namely affiliation to the Miners' Federation. Indeed, the Monmouthshire District Union had already joined the new organisation, and groups in other parts of the coalfield were seriously considering a similar course if the negotiations failed.

It was therefore surprising that a conference held in December finally resolved not to join the English miners in their campaign for a wage increase, and granted plenary powers to the negotiators.[8] This new moderate attitude, however, was very largely due to Mabon's influence, which was exerted to the full at this critical juncture. He unhesitatingly told the delegates that the men's demands, although admirable, were too numerous, and that they were seeking to build Rome in a day. His arguments throughout were in favour of the sliding scale, peaceful settlement and compromise. Mabon realised that an unyielding attitude was futile, since the Colliery Workmen's Federation was too weak to risk a stoppage, and the employers were firm in their refusal to concede all the far-reaching demands. On this as on other occasions, he frankly told the miners that they were adopting an unreasonable attitude, and although his bluntness made him unpopular for a while his views eventually triumphed. In spite of the anti-sliding scale elements his oratory finally carried the meeting, and armed with full powers to settle, Mabon returned to negotiate with the employers.

Largely owing to Mabon's skill as a negotiator the terms finally agreed included many of the clauses originally demanded by the men. The workmen were to receive a greater share in profits, the sliding scale was made more sensitive, and long contracts were excluded from the audits. Moreover the terms included a further bonus advance of $7\frac{1}{2}$ per cent, which placed wages in South Wales $2\frac{1}{2}$ per cent above the rates obtaining in the central coalfields of England. Thus many of the men's grievances concerning the sliding scale were met, and the arguments of the anti-sliding scale elements largely nullified. Despite the lack of enthusiasm with which it was received, there can be no doubt that the agreement of 1890 marked the high-water mark of the miners' achievements in the direction of modifying the sliding scale. From 1890 to 1898 the history of the sliding scale was the history of their struggle to preserve this agreement.

Unfortunately the Colliery Workmen's Federation was too weak to resist the coalowners' counter-attack, which developed when the period of high prices gave way to depression. Weakened by the efforts of the Miners' Federation to win recruits in South Wales, it proved powerless to resist the employers' demands. In June 1890 membership totalled only 28,000 men, and contributions to the central fund during the past year amounted to not more than £153. On a falling market, when the coalowners would be less unwilling to risk a stoppage, such a weak union could not hope to protect wages.

In the autumn of 1891 the employers served notice to terminate the agreement, and the negotiators were fortunate to preserve any of the gains won in 1890. As it was, they were forced to accept a reduction of $7\frac{1}{2}$ per cent in wages and a smaller share in the profits arising from any increase in coal prices. Moreover, they were forced to waive all claims to payment for small coal, the legality of which had been established by a series of test cases during the previous year. But as the Aberdare miners' leader observed, they were ' fortunate to have come out of such a hard struggle as well as they had, and . . . . had everyone done their duty regarding union . . . . in the past, things would not have gone as they did.'[9]

The men reopened negotiations in 1893 and again in 1895 in an attempt to regain the terms of 1890, but on both occasions they found the employers inflexible. It was almost solely due to Mabon's skill, and to the miners' willingness to allow him a free hand, that the final terms were in both cases the renewal of the agreement of 1892. The miners undoubtedly realised that their triumph of 1890 had been won by the pressures of the coal market rather than by their own efforts. On a falling market, when a stoppage would not involve the coalowners in great loss, the workmen's position was hopeless.

As Mabon and the other leaders realised, the formation of a strong union would at least do something to counterbalance the employers' advantage. But unfortunately the point was not well taken by the miners. When the Executive Committee attempted to increase union dues and build up a central fund in 1893, a delegate conference refused to do more than advise the Districts to comply. The failure of the sliding scale negotiations during the same year revived interest in the problem, and the union was reformed as the Amalgamated Association of Colliery Workmen of South Wales and Monmouthshire.[10] The rate of contribution was raised, and a greater proportion allocated to a central fund, from which strikes were to be financed. But once again the rank and file withheld their support, and in October 1893 Mabon could only compare the existing lack of organisation with the disorganisation of the years 1877 and 1879.[11]

It seems clear that the miners were not yet ready for the union of all South Wales which Mabon desired, and the weak District organisations remained paramount. But undoubtedly the progress of the union was further hindered by the efforts of the Miners' Federation of Great Britain to win recruits in the area through its Monmouthshire branch. It was, of course, futile for that organisation to advocate the replacement of the sliding scale by a conciliation board in Monmouthshire alone. Indeed, the employers generally refused to recognise the union. The only course was therefore to capture the whole of South Wales for the Miners' Federation, and this the Monmouthshire branch attempted to do under the able leadership of its miners' agent, William Brace.

Thus by the early 'nineties opinion in the coalfield was divided into two groups. One supported the destruction of the sliding scale and affiliation to the Miners' Federation, while the other favoured its retention and the formation of a strong local union. The first group, led by Brace, was small, while the latter, which followed Mabon, could claim much more support. But as Mabon observed, the conflict between the two schools of thought caused many men to ignore both and adopt a neutral attitude. As a result neither party could make much progress, and the effect upon unionism in the district as a whole was disastrous.

Undoubtedly the supporters of the sliding scale had the better case at this time. Wages had risen between 1888 and 1891, and the loss of the favourable terms of 1890 had been largely due to lack of organisation. It was obviously unwise to abandon the sliding scale until this situation was remedied. Moreover, as one of the men's leaders said, there appeared to be 'more blast and bluster than real worth' in connection with the Miners' Federation, which had achieved little. Wages in South Wales were higher than in the Federation areas until 1893, and the Federation had failed to resist substantial wage reductions in some coalfields.

The struggle between the two factions for control of the coalfield assumed its most violent form in August and early September of 1893. Hauliers employed in the Ogmore Valley stopped work, and the strike was extended by ' marching gangs' until almost all collieries were rendered idle. The stoppage was directed chiefly against the ' starving scale', and was largely influenced by the principles of the Miner's Federation. Resolutions were passed by the strikers demanding the abrogation of the agreement and affiliation to the Miners' Federation. A conference of the Federation's South Wales branches during July had resolved to seek a 20 per cent increase in wages, which was what the strikers demanded, and the pits at which the stoppage originated had just previously joined the Federation. Moreover, representatives of the Federation addressed and encouraged the strikers in the hope, it was alleged, of aiding the English coalfields, which were already idle, by reducing the supply of coal. Perhaps they merely used the existing discontent in an attempt to recruit members, but there is no doubt that the Miners' Federation was deeply implicated in the stoppage.

The coalowners, however, refused to negotiate with the strikers and withheld all pay due to them, while prosecuting the ringleaders for breach of contract. The presence of troops prevented intimidation, and since no strike pay was provided from any source the strike soon collapsed. Other workmen assumed the hauliers duties, and an increase in wages under the sliding scale in August robbed the strike of its main justification. Except in Monmouthshire, the colliers showed little sympathy with the hauliers. It was generally believed that the strike had been fomented by English workmen from Bristol and the Forest of Dean who had recently found work in South Wales. The Welsh miners for the most part held aloof, and blamed the strike on a ' gang of reckless hauliers'.

Meanwhile the sliding scale committee issued a manifesto condemning the stoppage as a dishonourable and illegal violation of the current agreement. Mabon himself reacted even more strongly, and was prominent in addressing meetings to the same effect, often at considerable personal danger. He emphasised that the stoppage was illegal and therefore indefensible, and his oratory was so convincing that, as one heckler observed, ' let Mabon call meetings like this and there is no success for the movement'.[12]   It is certainly safe to say that Mabon's influence over the workmen, especially those of Welsh origin, was a major cause of the collapse of the strike.

The immediate outcome of the stoppage was a change in the policy of the Federation, which had lost ground owing to its failure to win an advance in wages. In November 1893, Brace made a tacit admission that his efforts to win over members from the District Unions had failed. He approached the miners' leaders with a proposal that both parties should unite to create an effective organisation, independent of both the sliding scale and the Miners' Federation. Mabon, however, opposed the suggestion on the grounds that the local unions would have to be strengthened before going further, and the matter lapsed.[13] Brace's next step was to recognise that a majority of the miners still supported the sliding scale and advise his followers to pay the sliding scale levies. This would entitle them to attend the sliding scale conferences, where they could put their views in debate and still be free to advocate the principles of the Miners' Federation elsewhere.[14] This policy was speedily implemented, and from May 1894 the Federation's supporters proceeded to undermine the sliding scale from within.

More important, however, his temporary acceptance of the sliding scale principle enabled Brace to renew his proposals regarding unionism, and receive a more sympathetic hearing. In October 1894 he convened a ' Round Table Conference ' of miners' agents, which was attended by both supporters and opponents of the sliding scale. It seems likely that Brace wished the new organisation to be highly centralised and based upon large contributions to a central fund. But a conference called to consider the question clearly showed that the Districts were unwilling to lose their autonomy.[15] Consequently the Amalgamated Society of the Colliery Workmen of the South Wales Coalfield, which was established in November, differed little from the loose confederations of the past. In one direction it was even weaker than its predecessors, since the Rhondda miners and the colliers of the anthracite district refused to give it their support. The attitude of these two areas was largely due to

Mabon's hostility to the new union, for it was in these districts that his influence was greatest.

Mabon still believed that a just sliding scale was the best method of wage regulation. He was, of course, keenly interested in modifying the various agreements in the men's favour, but did not doubt that the sliding scale could be shaped into a nearly perfect mechanism. Whatever its defects, it had avoided disastrous stoppages and had given steadiness to trade and wages. Yet he realised that the sliding scale committee needed the support of a well-organised body of miners if they were to achieve the desired modifications. Despite the discouraging response, he had laboured unceasingly to weld the weak District unions into a powerful organisation which might later become part of a national association. The appearance of the Miners' Federation had hindered, if not entirely frustrated, his efforts. Its policy had little to commend it, since a conciliation board was only a sliding scale committee in effect, except that it left the employers free to press wage reductions at any time. Nor did he think it wise to join the Federation, since coalfields the conditions and markets of which differed from those of South Wales dictated its policies and frequently used the strike weapon. Even so, he and the other leaders had offered to join the Miners' Federation in 1890 and again in 1893 provided they were allowed to retain the sliding scale. But on this issue he remained inflexible.

His attitude towards the new union cannot, however, be explained solely in terms of hostility to the Miners' Federation. Mabon's disagreements with Brace over policy were perhaps less important than the personal antagonisms that had developed. The characters of the two men were so different that personal enmity had arisen as the dispute over the sliding scale became more bitter. They had much in common. Both were able men, both occasionally preached and both were largely self-educated. But at the time when the controversy raged Brace was still a young man in his twenties, while Mabon had already served the miners for a generation. Mabon's cautiousness irritated Brace, while Brace's enthusiasm and inexperience made him appear a hot-head in Mabon's eyes.

Moreover, Brace was altogether a more flamboyant personality than the older leader. As a result, the arguments between them were tinged with bitterness, and personal attacks became increasingly frequent, although Mabon, as always, criticised policies rather than persons.

In August 1893 Brace's attacks upon Mabon had resulted in a slander suit, which was heard at Swansea. Mabon had won the case and been awarded damages of £500. But he could not easily forget Brace's allegations, which were that

> ' he had betrayed the interests of the men who paid him and was secretly working in the interests of the employers and against the men, that he was acting in a corrupt and dishonourable manner as paid agent and representative and was not honestly and independently doing the best he could for the men who employed him, but had betrayed their interests and was in fact receiving money from the coalowners and working in concert with them'.[16]

As the new union was inspired by Brace, Mabon refused to support it, since ' he could not see his way clear to co-operate with men who had done everything they could, and left nothing undone, to place him and his family without any means of existence and who had slandered his character ; that without receiving an apology or some reparation he could not co-operate with those men'.[17] Meetings of the Cambrian Miners' Association and the anthracite colliers had endorsed his attitude, with the result that neither gave their support to the new organisation. Two further interesting points may be noted in passing. Mabon, in fact, never received the £500 damages which he was awarded, for Brace and his entire union could not raise the sum. And the coalowners, as a token of esteem for Mabon and opposition to the Miners' Federation, offered to pay £500 towards his legal expenses, although he apparently declined to accept this.

Mabon's hostility, however, was not the only reason for the failure of the new union. It was widely criticised as having been established by the leaders without adequate reference to the workmen's views. Moreover, Brace eventually confessed that his efforts to base the union on a central fund and uniform contributions had led to wholesale secessions. Indeed, this experience convinced him that a uniform contribution was impracticable unless it was equal to the smallest contribution paid to any District association in the coalfield. The organisation remained in existence until 1897, but its membership and influence seem to have been negligible. Until the strike of 1898 appeared imminent unionism remained a minor issue in the coalfield, the attention of the miners and their leaders being claimed by the question of wages.

From June 1894 to April 1897 wage rates, as determined by the sliding scale, fell steadily, and the immediate problem for Mabon and the other leaders was to halt or reverse this trend. Attempts to revise the sliding scale proved impossible, however, and the absence of any real union organisation precluded direct negotiation or the abandonment of the automatic wage regulator. Therefore Mabon reverted to the policy which he had advocated during the eighties, namely restriction of output. He undoubtedly realised by this time that the selling price of coal was not the sole indicator of the employers' ability to pay higher wages, since the volume of sales was equally important in determining profits. Moreover, the sliding scale encouraged the coalowners to sell cheaply, since wages would fall as prices were reduced, which, together with increased sales, would maintain profits. Thus Mabon saw the need for a minimum below which wages could not be reduced by the cut-throat competition for markets, or for some control over the actual selling price of coal.

As early as March 1894 Mabon persuaded a conference of miners to order strict observance of the nine-hour day in order to restrict output. But it was not until 1896 that a comprehensive scheme was proposed with the general support of the workmen. Realising that the employers were perhaps as hardpressed by the depression as the men, the miners' leaders devised a scheme which, with the coalowners help, would raise coal prices.

The scheme was to ensure fair profits and wages, so far as this was possible without raising prices to a non-competitive level, and was to be incorporated in the sliding scale agreement. Its main feature was that the men were to receive a minimum wage equal to the wage rates of 1879. This, taken with the average cost of production in the coalfield over the last three years, was to determine a minimum selling price for the various types of coal. The coalowners were left free to charge any price above this minimum, limited only by the existing market for coal.[18]

In practice the scheme would have proved difficult, if not impossible, to work. The prices would have been hard to calculate, for example, and the imposition of a more or less arbitrary price might have had serious repercussions on the demand for Welsh coal in a competitive market. If the minimum selling price was above what the market was willing to pay, the employers would have been forced to disregard it, or face bankruptcy. In any case, a price based on average costs over the past three years was unrealistic, since costs varied through time and from pit to pit, and were bound to be higher than average at many collieries, which would have to close down. But Mabon and the other leaders were mainly interested in securing a minimum wage, and worked on the assumption that under-cutting between the various coalowners in South Wales was the sole cause of the low prices. The problem remained of purely academic interest, however, for the owners, when presented with the scheme, pointed out that such an agreement would entail prosecution under the Conspiracy Act.

But the coalowners, too, were deeply concerned about the current low prices, and after examining various restriction schemes which had been adopted elsewhere decided to form a cartel. Their plan was substantially that proposed by D. A. Thomas (later Lord Rhondda), who attributed the depression to competition among the Welsh coalowners. His scheme proposed that each colliery should be entitled to produce a certain percentage of the total output of the district, this quota being based upon its current share of the market. In the future any firm exceeding its quota was to pay a fine on each excess ton, which would be paid as compensation to those firms who sold less than their quota. The agreement was to be legally binding on the parties concerned, who were nevertheless free to fix output and prices at their own discretion.[19] Thus it was highly flexible, and avoided the difficulties involved in the men's proposals.

The scheme did not include a minimum wage, but the attitude of the men's leaders was nevertheless favourable. Mabon, for example, expressed determination to win a minimum wage rate for the colliers but stated that he was prepared to give the scheme a fair trial.[20] This was the general view, and the coalowners' proposal was in fact also praised by the Miners' Federation and by the International Miners' Congress.

It was believed that the scheme would protect wages. But this was an error, since it did little to regulate prices, which were still the sole determinant of wages under the sliding scale. If employers chose to expand output and sell cheaply, the fall in wages associated with the lower price might well counterbalance the fines imposed, and increase profits. Indeed, the miners could probably be forced to pay the fines indirectly by reduced allowances or longer hours. In any case wages still depended upon how favourable the terms of the sliding scale agreement were to the men. Most serious of all, if the scheme raised prices it might reduce the market for Welsh coal, and unless it did raise prices it would prove valueless to the men.

Mabon, in fact, expected the scheme to raise coal prices by at least 1s. 0d. per ton, without considering whether this unnatural increase would harm the industry.[21] But the coalowners apparently came to realise that this would play into the hands of their competitors, for they took no immediate steps to put the plan into operation. Moreover, coal prices had begun to rise again of their own accord, so that the scheme became unnecessary. Finally in July 1897 they announced that the scheme was to be abandoned, on the grounds that too few coalowners favoured its adoption.

This decision sealed the fate of the sliding scale. The men had only refrained from terminating the agreement because they had hoped that the cartel would make it workable. Even Mabon recognised that there was need for a revision of its terms, and many miners felt that the whole principle of the sliding scale was unsatisfactory unless wages were guaranteed

in some way. The workmen were determined to win a
minimum wage either with or without a sliding scale. Coupled
with their bitter disappointment at the owners' attitude, this
augured ill for the peace of the coalfield.

Paradoxically only Mabon, the outstanding advocate of
output restriction, urged moderation. He in fact advised the
men not to press for the adoption of the scheme. The coalowners
were strongly opposing the Workmen's Compensation Bill,
then before parliament, on the grounds that it would raise coal
prices, and they could not adopt a scheme for artificially
increasing prices without destroying their case. Mabon's advice
was to wait until the Bill became law before re-opening the
question, for he felt that the miners could not hope to gain two
great blessings in the same year.[22] But even he could not stem
the tide. After four unsuccessful attempts to persuade the
owners to reconsider their decision, a conference held in
September 1897 finally resolved to serve notice to terminate the
agreement.

The decision was unfortunate. As Mabon no doubt knew,
the employers welcomed the opportunity to revise the agreement in their favour. They were alarmed by the rising cost of
coal production in the district, which was making Welsh coal
non-competitive in foreign markets. Low output per man,
refusal to work the double shift, and absenteeism were blamed
for this state of affairs, and the coalowners were determined to
find a remedy in lower wages. The workmen, on the other hand,
were equally firm that ' unless they got a better scale they
would do without one.' Indeed, a conference held early in
1898 ordered Mabon and the other leaders to draft a plan for
a new union of the entire coalfield. This decision came too late
to strengthen their position, of course, but showed that the
miners felt the seriousness of the situation and the possibility
of a stoppage.

VI

THE SOUTH WALES MINERS' FEDERATION

NEGOTIATIONS for the revision of the sliding scale were begun early in 1898, the men's main demand being the formation of a cartel or the inclusion of a minimum wage clause. The employers, however, pressed for an agreement less favourable to the men than that of 1892 and numerous other concessions, notably the abolition of Mabon's Day. Neither side was eager to compromise, and finally the negotiations broke down during March, when both parties rejected the other's proposals.[1]

Mabon's advice at this point was to drop the demand for a minimum wage and attempt to renew the existing agreement, rather than abandon the sliding scale principle and risk a stoppage. But the miners were not prepared to compromise, and demonstrated their firmness by withholding plenary powers from their representatives. Unfortunately the coalowners chose this crucial moment to announce that they would not treat with negotiators who lacked full power to settle. In a desperate attempt to save the situation, Mabon persuaded the employers to extend the notice of termination while a ballot was taken on the question of plenary powers. But with the expiration of the notice on 31 March, the workmen took matters into their own hands, and chose to disregard the extension. Few miners reported for work on 1 April, and as the strike became general it was announced that the ballot had shown an overwhelming majority against granting plenary powers.[2]

All hope of an early settlement had now disappeared. A conference on 7 April voted Mabon out of his position as chairman, demonstrating the rejection of his policy of compromise by the miners. Clearly no agreement would be acceptable to the men that did not incorporate a minimum wage, and on 12 April the employers issued a statement that this was one condition which they could not even discuss. As a result a further conference resolved on 18 April not to seek a renewal of the sliding scale, and stated that work might resume pending the negotiation of some other method of wage regulation. The coalowners, however, merely restated their position regarding plenary powers, and added that the pits would remain closed until a permanent settlement was reached.

But in time the hardship occasioned by the strike brought about the result which Mabon's oratory had failed to achieve. The funds of the District unions were soon exhausted, and an appeal to miners still working produced no real assistance. Late in April the Miners' Federation made a grant of £500 per week, but even this generous gesture meant little when most of the 128,000 men in the district needed relief. By May the colliers were dispirited and willing to end the dispute. One colliery after another voted in favour of granting plenary powers to the negotiators, and eventually a conference formally conferred such powers upon the miners' representatives. At this meeting the miners' chastened mood found expression when Mabon was once again elected chairman.[3]

Even with full powers to settle, however, Mabon was unable to end the stoppage immediately. The coalowners, realising the strength of their position, adopted a firm attitude, and even refused to meet a conciliator appointed by the government.[4] They would not consider a conciliation board agreement with provision for a minimum wage, which the men still demanded, and insisted that the selling price of coal should govern wages. During July they offered to re-employ workmen on the terms of the 1892 agreement provided Mabon's Day was abolished, and were prepared to grant a wage increase of 5 per cent by way of compensation. But this proposal was rejected by a miners' conference, which repeated the demand for a conciliation board agreement with a minimum wage clause. As Mabon observed :

> ' a new generation had been born which believed that wages in South Wales should be regulated on the same principle as were the wages of the major part of the colliers of the United Kingdom, who now held the opinion that wages should regulate the price of the commodity rather than that the price of the commodity should regulate wages'.[5]

The stoppage therefore continued, but during August resolutions were passed at various collieries in favour of accepting even a sliding scale, provided a minimum wage was guaranteed.

This was the policy which Mabon had advocated, and negotiations were re-opened on this basis. The employers now refused to consider any settlement other than that offered in July. But they were prepared to add a clause allowing the men to terminate the agreement if wages fell below 12½ per cent on the standard of 1879.

Mabon chose to regard this clause as a guarantee that the coalowners would not, in fact, reduce wages below this level. Brace, on the other hand, stated that the clause did not in any way constitute a minimum wage. But Mabon finally persuaded a conference held on 31 August to adopt his interpretation, and the employers' terms were accepted.[6] It was hoped that Mabon's Day could be saved, but when the coalowners remained adamant the new agreement was signed on 1 September.

The loss of Mabon's Day was a serious reverse, but as compensation there was the 5 per cent advance, and the final terms were certainly more favourable to the men than those offered before the strike. Moreover, it was generally believed that the minimum wage principle had been won, although the rate incorporated in the agreement was not sufficiently high to constitute a living wage. This was certainly Mabon's view, as we have seen. Whether the employers would, in fact, have paid the minimum wage if coal prices fell below the appropriate level remains uncertain. Fortunately the real value of the clause was never tested, for during the operation of the agreement wages did not fall so low as to reach the level of 12½ per cent above the 1879 rates.

By far the most significant outcome of the strike of 1898, however, was the realisation that lack of organisation and funds had forced the men to accept the owners' terms. Speaking of the negotiations, Mabon told the men that they 'would have to do the same as I have had to do today, namely to accept the inevitable and prepare to organise for better things'.[7] At last the rank and file were aroused from their apathy, and even those who disapproved of the settlement were wholeheartedly in favour of forming a strong union in South Wales. Thus the conference of 31 August which accepted the terms of settlement

also resolved that the provisional committee should formulate
a general scheme of organisation for the entire district. Moreover, it was also decided that each workman should contribute
1s. of his pay to the new union, 3d. of which was to be used to
form the nucleus of a central fund.

The miners' leaders were all agreed that the new union
should be based upon the pit-lodge system and voluntary
contributions. This in itself was a radical departure from the
procedure followed by most of the old District organisations,
and especially Mabon's Cambrian Miners' Association. But
he was by this time 'convinced by recent circumstances that
the sliding scale as a method of regulating wages was not the
best one. Its usefulness and value had gone. The new condition
of things demanded new measures, and after the end of the
present agreement no other sliding scale would be in operation
in the South Wales coalfield.'[8] This meant that the only
obstacle which had led him to oppose affiliation to the Miners'
Federation was removed, and so it was inevitable that the new
union would join that organisation. Indeed, by this time, as
Brace observed, 'the men were clamouring for national
Federation'. For this reason alone it was necessary to frame the
new organisation on the lines of the English unions, but even
more important was the realisation that the men's wages
would fairly soon depend solely upon their bargaining strength.

The South Wales Miners' Federation was formally established by a conference on 11 October 1898, Mabon being chosen
President.[9] Its structure was largely confederal, and despite
some reorganisation of boundaries the old Districts retained a
considerable proportion of each members' contribution. But
the adoption of the pit-lodge system and reliance upon voluntary contributions marked a new departure. Mabon was
perhaps doubtful that the men would accept these innovations,
for he stressed that they 'required to be educated in the
principles and methods of Trade Unionism'.[10] He launched an
intensive programme of meetings for this purpose, and took
pains to make it clear that non-unionists would not obtain the
services of the leaders or the organisation. Moreover, the union
served notice to terminate contracts at many collieries to force

non-unionists to become members or to win the closed shop. But the success of the new organisation was so instantaneous that his fears proved to be without foundation. By late December 1898 membership had reached sixty thousand men, showing that the miners now realised that their only hope of maintaining wages lay in organisation.

Meanwhile the Miners' Federation had made it clear that the new union could become affiliated at once, provided the Welsh miners agreed to abandon the sliding scale principle at the end of the current agreement. As a result Mabon led a deputation to a conference held at Edinburgh in January 1898. After some discussion, South Wales was admitted to the Federation and Mabon appointed to the national executive committee. In view of his previous opposition to the Miners' Federation many of its leaders must have been surprised at his changed attitude. But as he told the conference, the deputation came as ' three penitent Welshmen. They were the children of the resurrection, having found conviction by fact and harsh treatment.'[11]

For Mabon personally the years between 1898 and 1904 brought many honours and distinctions, although there was a noticeable deterioration in his health, which forced him to miss important conferences and led to a prolonged convalescence on the French Riviera in 1904.

During 1901 he accepted an invitation from a firm of Liverpool ship-owners to join a group of labour leaders on a tour of the industrial centres of the United States. The purpose of the visit was to study production methods and means of dealing with labour questions. Leaving England in October, accompanied by his youngest son, Mabon spent three months travelling through Ohio, Pennsylvania, New York State and Vermont. He arrived home at Liverpool on New Year's Day, 1902, with a mass of notes, observations and reminiscences, which were to provide material for many lectures and speeches. In nearly every town visited, Mabon had either lectured, preached or addressed the miners. Wherever he went he was given a princely reception, especially by the American Welshmen. He declared that he could not find words to describe the overwhelming kindness shown him everywhere, and quoted a remark made by Judge Edwards of Scranton that no Welshman had ever been received with greater enthusiasm. His tour through the Wyoming Valley from Wilkesbarre up to Carbondale seems to have been in the nature of a triumphal progress.[12]

During the winter of 1904–5, Mabon again visited the United States, this time as a delegate from the Trade Union Congress to the American Federation of Labour Congress at San Francisco. He was able to stop at many towns on the route from New York to the Pacific Coast, often as the guest of local trade unions, and he appears to have repeated his former triumph. Of his speech at the Congress it was said that ' he gave one of the most concise outlines of the English labour problem that has ever been told on the floor of a Federation convention'.[13] Much of his time was given to advocating conciliation as a means of avoiding disputes in American industry, for he admitted that he hoped to influence public opinion in this direction. His speeches received considerable attention in the American press, and one address delivered in Colorado is especially interesting as a summary of his views on industrial relations.

> ' If his conscience did not justify his advocacy of the labour question he would drop the question at once. They were working to elevate the working man, to give him an opportunity to prove himself worthy of all he asked for and all that could be given him. A fair day's work for a fair day's wage was right, but he demanded of them that they should give a fair day's work for a fair day's wages. They had found a better way to fight out these questions than by strikes and lock-outs. The days of those weapons should be no more. They were unnecessary. The man that won lost, and the man that lost sustained a double loss. (In South Wales) our shrapnel and shot are facts and figures, and our battles are fought around a table'.[14]

Meanwhile the International Miners' Congress at Dusseldorf during May, 1902, had elected Mabon general treasurer in succession to Thomas Burt, who had resigned. That Mabon was thought worthy to succeed the Grand Old Man of mining unionism was in itself a great honour. But early in 1904, Mabon was also appointed treasurer of the Miners' Federation of Great Britain, during a re-shuffle of the executive caused by the death of Benjamin Pickard. Thus it is clear that by this time Mabon was known and respected throughout the United Kingdom and even abroad. Yet as always his main concern was the well-being of the colliery workmen in South Wales.

In the years that followed the strike of 1898, Mabon threw himself wholeheartedly into the task of completing the organisation of the Welsh miners. Much was achieved by persuasion, but owing to the workmen's changed attitude towards unionism other methods were also feasible. At many collieries the union threatened or brought about stoppages, in an attempt to force non-unionists into the organisation. But although membership increased as a result, such stoppages were expensive, and the union's finances suffered accordingly in these early years. Substantial deficits appeared in 1904 and 1905 and only very small surpluses in 1903 and 1906. One reason for this was that the miners still refused to pay large union dues, the rate of contribution in South Wales being only half that levied by English organisations. This was to remain, as it had been in the past, a most serious problem, which even Mabon was unable to solve. But despite weak finances, the new federation showed that it was determined to adopt an aggressive policy on the question of wages. Almost from its inception the union's attitude revealed that the miners would use their growing strength to maintain wage rates, even though the sliding scale remained in force.

On 9 November 1900, and on five occasions in the autumn of 1901, the union executive ordered a general holiday in the coalfield. These ' stop days', which were an attempt to restrict output, came as a surprise to the employers, since wages in the industry were higher than ever before. Moreover, Mabon admitted that the miners did not believe that it was possible or even desirable to keep coal prices at the current famine level. The ' stop days' were, in fact, intended as a warning to buyers who had been ' holding the market altogether or making contracts for three months only . . . in the hope or belief that prices would give way'. Their purpose, as Mabon explained in a catchy jingle, was

> To kill the ring that caused the slump
> To throttle the thing — bring it down with a thump

Unfortunately the coalowners, while admitting that something should be done about the middlemen's manipulations,
regarded the union's cure as worse than the disease. Protests
were made to the miners' leaders after the solitary ' stop day '
called in 1900. But when the policy was revived in 1901 despite
their warnings, the employers chose to sue the union in the
courts. Initially the case was intended to establish the illegality
of such stoppages and prevent their recurrence. As time passed,
however, more and more stress was laid upon the question of
damages, and after an appeal to the House of Lords the union
was eventually forced to pay £57,000 as compensation. The
claim for damages was perhaps pressed in the knowledge that
if successful the union's finances and bargaining power would
be seriously affected. But the proceedings are of especial interest
since they involved the novel principle established by the Taff
Vale Decision, that a union's funds could in fact be attacked
in this way. It would appear that the miners' organisation was
the first union in South Wales to feel the effects of this ruling.

While Mabon and the miners were fighting the merchants
and coalowners to protect their wage rates, they were also called
upon to do battle with the government on the same issue.
During 1901 it became known that a tax of 1s. per ton was to be
imposed upon coal exports from the United Kingdom. Since
South Wales was primarily an exporting district both the miners
and the coalowners reacted violently to this measure. The
employers complained that under such a burden Welsh coal
would fail to find buyers in the highly competitive foreign
market, with bankruptcy and unemployment as the inevitable
outcome. But Mabon was more concerned that the coalowners
might shift such a tax onto the miners by reducing their
earnings in some way. By April 1901 he was ' seriously considering the advisability of . . . a stoppage not merely of the
South Wales coalfield but of (all) the steam coal miners within
the Miners' Federation of Great Britain'.[16] His attitude was
wholeheartedly supported by the rank and file, and when the
Miners' Federation discussed the question it was a South Wales
delegate that seconded the motion for a strike. But on this
occasion Mabon found himself in the unusual role of an

extremist, for most of the coalfields included in the Miners' Federation voted against a stoppage. Although he was convinced that ' it was a mistake not to have carried out that resistance (to the tax) to the very end' South Wales could not act alone.[17] The non-exporting coalfields were not vitally interested in the matter, and opposition to the tax was confined to constitutional means until its repeal in 1906.

The stop days and the question of the tax on coal, however, were merely attempts to safeguard wages within the framework of the sliding scale. The real test of the union's strength came during 1902, when the four year period for which the agreement was binding came to an end. A conference held in July of that year resolved, not unexpectedly, to serve notice of termination. But although this step had been inevitable since affiliation to the Miners' Federation, even the workmen's leaders were surprised by the unanimity displayed. As Mabon observed, it was attributable to a realisation that a sliding scale was valueless without a minimum wage clause, and to the harsh terms forced on the men in 1898.

In November 1902 the union began negotiations with the employers. The objective was to replace the sliding scale by a conciliation board, which would determine wages between certain minimum and maximum levels. Bowing to the inevitable, the employers were prepared to accept these proposals in principle. But they demanded a wage reduction as a *quid pro quo*. Moreover, they insisted that the selling price of coal should remain a factor in the determination of wages by the board, and that an equivalent selling price to the minimum wage should be set at 11s. This meant, in effect, that the principle of the sliding scale would be retained, since conciliation board agreements in other coalfields included no such clauses. Since the minimum wage principle had been accepted, the miners' only objection to the proposals was that the equivalent selling price ought to be fixed at 11s 3d. It had been traditional in South Wales that prices should be a factor in setting rates, and it is probable that Mabon, at least, favoured this approach. But the union was determined not to accept any wage reduction or an excessively low minimum wage level. At this stage both parties reached the limits of their concessions, and a deadlock ensued that threatened to repeat the events of 1898.[18]

On this occasion, however, Mabon enjoyed the confidence of the miners, and could concentrate his powers of persuasion upon the employers. As complete breakdown of the negotiations became imminent he proposed recourse to arbitration ' in a speech brimful of force and eloquence', urging the owners ' to hesitate again and again before they finally spurned this offer '. The suggestion was finally accepted for, as one union delegate remarked, ' our old man was at his very best — he seemed really inspired, (and) in every word he uttered a tear'.[19]

But Mabon's difficulties were not yet over, for the employers were only prepared to adopt his solution provided the conciliation board agreement was made binding for three years. The men's representatives did not object, in view of the favourable terms. The Miners' Federation, however, had decided that all districts should be free to act together on the question of wages at the end of 1903. If the employers' proposals were accepted South Wales would not be able to join in this campaign, and the attitude of the Welsh leaders was severly criticised at a conference of the Federation. Once again the burden fell upon Mabon, who gave ' his version of the story and . . . . was never heard in better form. Cool and cautious, studiously declining to be provoked to anger, he recounted clearly and with deliberation the facts that had faced them in South Wales during the negotiations. Those facts were martialled with the skill of a diplomatist, and the conference was visibly impressed.'[20] Convinced by his arguments that no other solution was possible, the Miners' Federation granted South Wales a free hand in the matter. As a result the first conciliation board agreement to become operative in the coalfield was signed on 31 March 1903.

The soundness of Mabon's policy in this difficult situation was demonstrated in December 1905. On this occasion the agreement was renewed for a further four years without consulting the Miners' Federation, which was again trying to bring about a concerted wage policy for all districts. Apparently the miners realised that a favourable agreement safely signed was preferable to the uncertainties involved in attempts to regulate wages at the national level. With a minimum wage rate guaranteed they did not object to the establishment of an equivalent selling price or to the principle that coal prices should affect wage rates. In practice wages under the concilia- tion board moved with coal prices in much the same way as under the sliding scale. The only real difference was that the correlation between wages and prices was not quite as close, owing to the relatively infrequent meetings of the board and the occasional refusal of the chairman to award the change demanded.

But if the miners were satisfied with the agreement, the general public were equally appreciative of Mabon's role as peacemaker. As Richard Lewis of Tonypandy expressed it in a letter to the *South Wales Daily News*, the coalfield owed much to Mabon :

> ' Inasmuch as the crisis is happily over and the recent deliberations of masters and men . . . have been brought to a satisfactory conclusion . . . now is the fitting moment for South Wales to rise to the occasion by giving a practical proof on a worthy scale of its appreciation of a man who, whilst invariably holding fast with grim tenacity to what he thought was right and just in the miners' interests, never said nor insinuated anything which might tend in the slightest degree to cause irritation or give offence to the employers of labour. Such men, when placed in positions of responsibility, are of inestimable value to the community at large. Indeed, I feel sure that I am voicing the opinion of a multitude of people today when I say there exists a strong desire on the part of all sorts and conditions of men to bestow upon Mabon, in the evening of his life, a busy and eventful one, a tangible expres- sion of regard and indebtedness for his long and valuable services in the industrial world'.[21]

The suggestion was warmly supported in the editorial columns of the *South Wales Daily News* and the *Western Mail*, and a public meeting at Cardiff on 1 May, 1903, launched a testimonial fund. Subscriptions immediately began to arrive from miners, coalowners, tradesmen and private persons all over South Wales. When the presentation was finally made in

March, 1905, Mabon received an inscribed silver salver and a
cheque for nearly £2,000.[22]

Undoubtedly the success of the testimonial fund was due to a
general and widespread recognition of the service which Mabon
had rendered to the community through his advocacy of peaceful settlement. But in the opinion of many such a policy was
beginning to appear outdated as politics and the class-war came
to influence the miners' views. Even as the tributes to his work
as a labour leader were conferred upon him, circumstances were
developing which were to end his supremacy in South Wales.

In September, 1899, the Trades Union Congress had
resolved that its political committee should invite all interested
bodies to confer on the problem of increasing the number of
workers' representatives in the House of Commons. As a result
the Labour Representation Committee came into being during
1900, comprising delegates from the Fabian Society, the Social
Democratic Federation, the Independent Labour Party and
some twenty small trade unions. For many reasons the Miners'
Federation had held aloof from this new body. It seemed to
have little to offer, since the miners' unions were already
supporting candidates both in elections and in Parliament. In
the circumstances affiliation to the Committee would merely
allow other organisations to take advantage of the finances and
strength of the Miners' Federation. The Liberal leaders of the
Federation mistrusted the scheme, since it drew much of its
support from such radical bodies as the Social Democratic
Federation and the Independent Labour Party. And in any
case they did not believe that the miners' political objectives
could be achieved except with the co-operation of the two
great political parties.

Even so, an increase in political activity was clearly desirable.
In 1902 the Miners' Federation implemented a scheme to
finance parliamentary action, based upon a monthly contribution of 1s. per member. A ballot taken in South Wales showed
that a majority of the miners supported the Federation's plan,
and Mabon was wholeheartedly in its favour. With such a fund,
he pointed out, some fifty members could be returned ' to
advocate the policy of the Federation on the floor of the House'.

They would have 'no more Home Secretaries turning a deaf ear to the legislative requirements of the miners, (whereas) if this course were not pursued, mining legislation apparently would be coming to a standstill'.[23]

In view of the effects of the Taff Vale Decision upon the union and the continuance of the export tax on coal, it was not surprising that the South Wales miners were enthusiastic supporters of the Federation's scheme. Indeed, they were the first to put it into effect, contesting the West Monmouthshire division in the by-election caused by the death of Sir William Harcourt in 1904. The miners' choice was Thomas Richards, the union's secretary, who stood as Labour and Progressive candidate. At a cost of only £1,332 to the organisation he was elected by a majority of 4,635 votes over his Conservative opponent.[24] From this triumph the union went on to contest the general election of 1906, and in addition to Richards successfully supported Mabon in the Rhondda, Brace in South Glamorgan and John Williams in Gower.

But meanwhile the Labour Representation Committee had rapidly increased its strength, so that a movement developed among the miners in favour of affiliation to that body. This minority was vocal at conferences of the Miners' Federation, and eventually forced a ballot on the question in 1906. Fundamentally the choice lay between the Federation's scheme, with its implied allegiance to the Liberal party, and the Labour Representation Committee, which stood for an independent working class party. The ballot of 1906 showed a majority of 9,492 in favour of the former policy, but a further ballot taken in 1908 reversed this decision by over 44,000 votes. As a result the Miners' Federation finally became affiliated to the Labour Party, as the Labour Representation Committee had now become, during 1909.

The executive committee of the South Wales miners' union was sharply divided on the question of labour representation. So evenly were the numbers divided that no recommendation was made to the workmen in the ballot of 1906, since Mabon refused to give his casting vote.[25] But he nevertheless made his views on the matter very clear. He acted as spokesman for the faction that favoured the Liberal connection rather than affiliation to the Socialist movement. As he put it:

> ' when the day came for these movements to be one move-
> ment, if Mabon was alive he would be there ; . . . the only
> difference between him and his friends was that they . . .
> believed that to be independent of all parties was the best
> policy, even if they had to wait some time before they reached
> the goal (while) he believed in making use of friends on the way
> (since) no measure could be got in the House without votes'. [26]

He did not believe that a policy of isolation could be successful, and many of the union executive agreed with his contention.

But Mabon and his supporters found that their allegiance to the Liberal party was unpopular in the coal-field. In the ballot of 1906 a majority of the South Wales miners voted for affiliation to the Labour Representation Committee, although a large number abstained. Socialism had taken root in the area, partly through the efforts of Keir Hardie, but largely owing to the support given to the strikers in 1898 by the Independent Labour Party. At the close of this strike, which ' was not unfruitful politically ', thirty-one branches of the party existed in South Wales, chiefly in the Merthyr and Rhondda districts. [27] Since that time the Independent Labour Party and the less popular Social Democratic Federation had been engaged in disseminating Socialist propaganda on a large scale.

Yet the movement for an independent Labour party was not entirely the result of Socialist agitation. As Mabon confessed, the miners now realised the power of the vote, and the Socialist successes were mainly due to the ' feeling of so many working people that they were only tolerated (in Parliament) and allowed a voice on sufferance ' by the major political parties. [28]

Even Mabon's influence could not sway the men. It was the South Wales miners who, at their annual conference in 1907, decided to force another ballot upon the Miners' Federation. The motion was discussed by a Federation conference at Southport, and bitter attacks were made upon the trade union members of Parliament. It was contended that the only true friends of the working classes were the Labour Party presided over by Keir Hardie, and that the trade union members were

bound hand and foot to the Liberal party. Nor was the accusation entirely without foundation. The trade union members
were treated in a cavalier manner by the Liberals, who assumed
that their votes could always be relied upon. Mabon, despite
his faith in co-operation with the Liberal machine, was forced
to admit that ' they had not done all they would like to have
done'.[29] His argument of political expediency fell on deaf ears,
and in the ballot of 1908 the South Wales miners voted in
favour of affiliation to the Labour Party by a majority of thirty
thousand. This time, too, a majority of the entire Federation
also supported this policy, and application was made for
admission to the Labour Party. Mabon was one of a deputation
chosen to arrange final details with the Party, and early in 1909
the Federation became affiliated.

It may be noted in passing that the question of political
action involved the South Wales miners' union in expensive
and protracted litigation. The union's levy for political purposes
was the subject of court actions almost from its inception, most
of which were inspired by various Conservative organisations.
In February 1905 an Aberafan collier, A. G. Steele, had sought
an injunction at Newport County Court to restrain the union
from collecting or spending funds for political objectives. An
earlier case heard at Tredegar in 1905 had not been pressed.
But Steele, having lost the case on the grounds that he was
under no duress to pay the levy, appealed unsuccessfully to the
Divisional Court in January 1907.[30] Two years later one
Robert Butcher of Pen-y-graig sought a similar injunction at
Mountain Ash County Court.[31] The court granted the injunction in his case, but would not extend it to cover all members
of the union. Yet the Rhondda Conservative Association chose
to contest this wider issue, and since the Osborne Judgement
governed the point at issue a general injunction was granted in
July 1909. Until the reversal of the Osborne Judgement in
1913 the union was forced to rely upon voluntary contributions,
but the response was satisfactory, and its political activities
suffered little from the legal obstacles.

For Mabon, however, the result of the ballot of 1908 constituted a serious reverse. His influence had undoubtedly been

thrown against affiliation to the Labour Party, but had failed to affect the outcome. As a convinced Liberal he was forced to abandon his party and join an organisation with whose aims he had little sympathy. But most important of all, his views on the question had proved different from those held by the miners. It was an indication that he had lost touch with the rank and file, and that a strong socialist element existed in the coalfield. Their opinions on industrial matters would inevitably be at variance with those held by Mabon. Such concepts as the class war between labour and capital, nationalisation and other ideas quite foreign to Mabon's philosophy would rapidly become current in the coalfield. In short, his defeat on the political issue foretold that he would soon be faced with revolt among the rank and file of the union, and his policies overthrown.

8 Hours Act

THE NEW UNIONISM

THE year 1908 opened auspiciously for the Welsh miners and for Mabon. Wages were high, indeed higher than ever before under the conciliation board, and employment was plentiful in the coalfield. The union's numerical strength was at a peak as a result of vigorous campaigns against non-unionists, and its finances were correspondingly sound. Mabon and the executive committee were firmly in control of the organisation, and industrial peace seemed assured.

But in the same year two events occurred whose repercussions were soon to plunge the coalfield into unprecedented ferment. One, the passage of the Eight Hours Bill through Parliament, was hailed as a triumph by the workmen. The other, an unsuccessful court case fought by the union, appeared as an insignificant reverse. It could not have been foreseen that the problems to which these events gave rise were shortly to over-throw Mabon and his policies, almost destroy the union, and win for South Wales the reputation of being a storm centre of industrial strife.

The Eight Hours Act was greeted with enthusiasm in the coalfield. Miners in South Wales worked at least an hour longer than workmen in other districts each day, and had sought legislative reduction of working time since 1888. They therefore had more to gain from the Act than their fellow-workers else-where, and were perhaps proportionately more interested in its enactment. But of necessity the South Wales coalowners stood to lose an important cost advantage if the Bill became law, and they opposed it in parliament, in manifestos to the miners and in the press.

As was to be expected, Mabon appeared in the forefront of the controversy, maintaining that the social and physical well-being of the Welsh miners demanded a shorter working day.[1] But he, like the majority of the miners, neglected to stress

that a curtailed working shift would probably mean smaller
earnings under the prevalent piece-work system. The Departmental Committee on an Eight Hours Working Day in Mines
had given warning during 1907 that in ' South Wales . . . .
it is clear that by no re-arrangement of their time or improvement in the regularity of attendance could the hewers . . .
earn the same wages'.[2] Yet Mabon and the workmen apparently trusted to the union's strength and the conciliation board
mechanism to maintain the level of earnings. In their determination to avoid a fall in wages and to reduce working hours,
however, lay a major threat to the future peace of the coalfield.
Few miners could cut as much coal in eight hours as they had
previously done in nine or ten hours. Since each was paid on
the basis of the number of tons that he produced, earnings
would be bound to fall unless the payment per ton was increased. The employers, of course, were not likely to raise the
wage rate in this way when the Act came into force, for it
would mean that they were paying the same wage as previously
in return for a smaller output.

The court case, whose outcome was announced in January,
1908, had begun during the previous year. One Morgan
Walters of Ynys-y-bŵl, financed by the union, had sued the
Ocean Company ' to recover the difference in his earnings
through being employed in an abnormal place at the Lady
Windsor colliery'.[3] His grievance was by no means unusual in
the district, where physical conditions in many seams prevented
the collier from cutting as much coal as he would have done
under better circumstances. It had become the general practice
for colliery managers to pay a bonus or allowance over and
above the normal piece-rate, in order to compensate the collier
for his difficult working place. But such allowances were not
part of the miner's contract, and some employers, faced with
rising production costs, chose to economise by reducing these
bonuses. The decision in this test case, given at Pontypridd by
Judge Bryn Roberts, was that such allowances were not
recoverable in law, being ' a matter of gratuity'. It ran contrary
to the decisions given in similar suits by Judge Roberts' pre-
decessor, and marked a new departure. The coalowners were

now free to reduce allowances without fear of interference from the courts. When this occurred the workman who found himself in an abnormal working place could only maintain his level of earnings by working overtime ; and under the Eight Hours Act overtime would be limited by law. The so-called ' Sixty Hours ' clause allowed miners to work a number of longer shifts. But the total of extra working time over and above the basic eight hours per day was not to exceed sixty hours in any year.

No union could leave the earnings of its members to the whim of the employers, and Mabon immediately brought the matter to the attention of the conciliation board. A sub-committee discussed the problem during 1908, but failed to reach agreement.[4] As a result it was necessary to make provision for workmen in abnormal places part of the conciliation board agreement, and thus circumvent Judge Roberts' decision. During March 1909 a conference of the union resolved that the next agreement must guarantee ' colliers who worked in such places minimum earnings of not less than 4s. 9d. per day'.[5] The decision, although reasonable, was significant for the future peace of the coalfield. It showed that the miners, not content with a minimum wage rate, now sought a minimum level of earnings. From demanding such an arrangement for a special class of men to demanding it for all colliery employees would be only a short step.

During the next two years the union and the employers were engaged in a hopeless attempt to solve the problems arising from the Eight Hours Act and Judge Roberts' decision. Broadly speaking, the employers required freedom to work their pits in the most economic way. Their objective was to reduce costs so as to compensate for the fall in output arising from the Act, and thus keep selling prices competitive. In other words, they sought to keep production as high as possible and costs per ton as low as they had been in the past. This meant the introduction of new working methods, more rigid discipline and operation of the mines for the maximum time permitted by the Act. The workmen, on the other hand, were reluctant to work more than eight hours a day, and were suspicious of all new methods.

Moreover, they demanded a guaranteed wage for workmen in abnormal places, and sought desperately for any device that would enable the miners to maintain their level of earnings despite the shorter shift.

In view of the incompatibility of the aims of the two parties it is not surprising that they failed to settle the matters in dispute. Indeed, it is only surprising that they attempted to do so without recourse to industrial warfare. To a very great extent this was due to Mabon's restraining influence upon the miners and his abhorrence of the strike weapon. Despite a noticeable hardening of the employers' attitude, Mabon continued to press his conciliatory policy, choosing to compromise on almost any point rather than risk a stoppage. But in doing so he had now to contend not only with the coalowners but with discontented elements within the union. A growing faction regarded his efforts to preserve peace in the coalfield as weakness, his willingness to compromise as cowardice. A feeling developed among the workmen that the union was sufficiently strong to adopt a militant, aggressive policy and assert rather than negotiate for their rights.

The conflict between the union and the employers centred around the revisions of the conciliation board agreement in 1909 and 1910. During March 1909 the coalowners announced that the implementation of the Eight Hours Act on 1 July would, in their opinion, abrogate the existing agreement, and suggested that negotiations be opened to modify its terms. Some of their proposals, such as the abolition of mealtimes during shifts and of bonus payment for night work, were perhaps reasonable. But in addition they demanded the adoption of the double-shift system, which the South Wales miners had opposed for over fifty years and could not accept. Moreover, as mentioned above, the Eight Hours Act permitted miners to work a number of longer shifts, provided the hours worked in excess of eight per day did not total more than sixty hours in each year. The employers wished to compel the miners to work this extra time, and once again the workers' representatives were forced to object, partly as a matter of principle and partly because the Miners' Federation had ruled that the

' Sixty Hours ' clause must be ignored. Faced with a complete break-down of the negotiations Mabon appealed to the Miners' Federation for support, but when this was not forthcoming an agreement was hastily signed on 30 June.[6]

In order to avert a stoppage Mabon and the other representatives accepted almost all the employers' demands, without obtaining any important concessions in return. For example, the coalowners were allowed to adopt ' any new method of working their collieries without being met with the objection that their doing so is a breach of custom or of the conciliation board agreement'. It was decided to resolve the dispute regarding the sixty hours clause by means of a test case, a suggestion put forward by Mabon which contributed materially to the conclusion of a new agreement. Unfortunately, by some oversight he and his colleagues failed to notice that the conciliation board agreement contained a clause ' that the hours of labour shall be such as are authorised by the Coal Mines Regulation Act of 1908'. Since the Act clearly authorised the additional sixty hours the employers were certain to win the test case. When Messrs. Insoles Ltd. claimed 2s. 6d. damages for breach of contract from a miner who had refused to work a nine-hour shift during August, the court inevitably found for the plaintiffs. An appeal to the Divisional Court in December failed, and the coalowners pressed their advantage by demanding a total of £400,000 damages from all employees who had not worked the nine hour shift.[7]

The agreement of 1909 was therefore in need of revision almost as soon as it had been signed. Unless the miners were prepared to work the extra hours or pay damages for not doing so, the clause quoted above would have to be deleted. But as time passed some modification was made even more vital owing to the effects of the eight hour day upon earnings.[8] Working time fell by as much as 21 per cent as a result of the Act, and in the last quarter of 1909 average output per man decreased by up to 13 per cent, which involved a corresponding fall in earnings. The workmen engaged in abnormal places faced genuine hardship owing to the abolition of overtime, and hauliers, riders and trafficmen, the lowest paid workers in the mines, were perhaps even more severely affected.[9] At the same time friction developed as the employers introduced new methods of working, notably a Saturday afternoon shift, and as a final blow the conciliation board announced a reduction in the wage rate in March and June.

For all these reasons Mabon clearly expressed the general view when he stated during August that the conciliation board agreement would have to be revised to include ' a minimum wage for abnormal places and the raising of the standard wages of several classes of workmen'. He ' did not want the men to be too sanguine that they were going to get all they asked for in the next agreement,' but even so a lengthy table of demands was drafted during November.[10]

One significant proposal was that an umpire be appointed to settle disputes not resolved by the conciliation board, an indication that the board was failing in its efforts at conciliation. But all the others were concerned directly or indirectly with the miners' earnings, revealing the main source of discontent. They included a raising of the minimum wage rate to 40 per cent above the rates of 1879, payment for small coal and payment of a bonus shift to night workers. Most important of all, however, it was proposed that the lowest paid workmen and workmen in abnormal places should earn a minimum of 3s. 4d. and 4s. 9d. per day respectively.[11] These two demands constituted the first official recognition of the case for a universal minimum level of earnings, and marked a new departure in the union's policy.

When negotiations opened in January 1910 the employers produced an equally impressive list of proposals, all designed to reduce costs of production by lowering wages, lengthening the working day and introducing new methods in the mines. Moreover, their only concession on the question of abnormal places was that a miner dissatisfied with the allowances paid might be allowed to leave the pit without notice unless offered a normal working place. They firmly refused to guarantee a minimum level of earnings to any class of workman, on the grounds that it would remove the differential between good and bad employees and encourage slow working.

Obviously the union's efforts to increase earnings were diametrically opposed to the employers' intention of lowering costs. At the same time both sides were being driven to adopt an increasingly intransigent attitude by the effects of the eight hour day. The miners, for example, refused to grant plenary powers to Mabon and their other representatives, in an attempt to ensure that no compromise settlement was reached. It was clear by this time that the older leaders, and especially Mabon, would find it more and more difficult to preserve their policy of conciliation in the face of rising discontent within the union.

Eventually a stoppage was averted when a ballot of the workmen showed a large majority in favour of accepting the draft initialled by their representatives. A new agreement was signed on 8 April 1910, but once again it favoured the employers. By its clauses they were allowed to introduce the after noon shift, an overlapping shift and even the hated double-shift system in certain circumstances. The question of the sixty hours clause and the damages involved was dropped, but the employers were permitted to lengthen the short Sunday night shift to the full eight hours.[12] All that the workmen gained was an increase in the minimum wage rate to 35 per cent above the rates of 1879, which was valueless, since wage rates never fell below 50 per cent on the standard during the operation of the agreement.

Even from Mabon's point of view the only virtue of the new agreement was that it had averted a strike or lock-out. His sole justification for accepting it was that the terms were the ' very best that can be got at present from the South Wales coal-owners ' and included ' some advantages beyond what, honestly speaking, the most sanguine among us expected to receive'.[13] But while this was undoubtedly true, a miner who was facing real financial hardship might be expected to take a less rational attitude if the agreement failed to ameliorate his condition.

As was to be expected, the operation of the agreement produced a wave of unrest in the coalfield. Earnings had not been increased, the question of abnormal places had not been

solved, and a steady rise in the cost of living accentuated the
effects of the eight hour day upon the miners' pay. The employers, in their efforts to lower costs, began to withdraw minor
concessions which the men had enjoyed for decades, such as the
custom of taking home waste timber for use as firewood. Older
workmen were dismissed, all payments not included in the
price lists were reduced, and deductions made from miners'
wages on various pretexts. Colliers who had been involved in
disputes and had found work elsewhere were often traced by
their former employers and dismissed. Such disputes became all
too frequent, owing to the absence of a third party on the
conciliation board who could arbitrate upon minor problems.
As Mabon observed, the employers were ' breaking every
canon of the law of liberty in a free country ' while ' the
workmen and their families (experienced) shortages in the
real means of sustenance'.[14]

Under the pressures released by the Eight Hours Act the
entire machinery of the conciliation board was in fact breaking
down. Both employers and workmen found themselves sub-
jected to economic forces that made it impossible for them to
compromise or make concessions. Negotiations at colliery level
or for the coal-field as a whole became increasingly bitter and
hard-fought. Mabon's oratory and powers of persuasion could
no longer influence the course of events, for both miners and
coalowners had reached the limit beyond which concessions
could not be made. The atmosphere of mutal respect and con-
sideration essential to the success of Mabon's methods had
given way to fundamental distrust and hostility. And as soon as
his methods failed to produce results it was inevitable that his
position as unchallenged leader of the miners became insecure.

Undoubtedly the agreement of 1910 drove hundreds of
miners out of the union, as was reflected by a steady fall in
membership between 1909 and 1912. The impoverished
colliers had neither the time nor the money to support an
organisation that had failed to protect their interests. Within
the union executive younger leaders appeared, elected by the
discontented workers, who demanded the adoption of a fighting
policy in place of fruitless conciliation. Many indeed were

socialists or syndicalists, whose philosophy of the class war made it impossible for them to accept Mabon's views. But in any case their policy, in practice, was to attack Mabon and his attitude on various matters, in the hope of gaining control of the union and using it as an effective weapon in industrial warfare. During 1910 the clashes between the older leaders and this new element became so bitter that the union executive was forced to pass a resolution condemning any further public controversy regarding policy.[15]

The increasing influence of the younger leaders and the unrest among the miners found open expression during the summer and autumn of 1910. At Maesteg the workmen refused to pay any further union dues ; in the Aberdare district an unofficial strike occurred against the Powell-Duffryn Company. Most important of all, on 1 November the employees of the Cambrian Combine in the Rhondda Valley stopped work after tendering the necessary notice. It was this strike, which continued until September 1911, that finally broke Mabon's hold over the miners, the union, and its policy.

All these outbreaks had the support of the younger leaders, and were characterised by criticism of the union and its officials. James Winstone, a miners' agent from Pontnewydd, for example, expressed the following views on the Maesteg situation : ' the federation is much too tame (and) has, through the medium of the conciliation board, become practically inert as a fighting force. Instead of trying to reconcile capitalism and labour it should show the impossibility of such a reconciliation '.[16] Similar opinions were held by Vernon Hartshorn, the conciliation board representative for Maesteg : ' If the present policy of drift was allowed to go on — if the policy of the federation was left very much longer in the hands of the executive — the workmen would be absolutely at the mercy of the employers. A certain amount of wiping out must be done on the executive committee '.[17] C. B. Stanton, who led the Aberdare strikers, went even further. The older leaders had 'done some good in their day, but (they) must move on or move out ',[18] since ' the faint-hearted, over-cautious, creeping, crawling, cowardly set who pose as leaders but do not lead are responsible for the rotten condition of things today '.[19]

Mabon, whose influence had more than once swayed the miners, was perplexed by this ' spirit of insubordination and open defiance of the responsible officials'. His only explanation was that it arose from ' the severe struggle between the old and sane trade unionism and the new socialistic unions.'[20] No doubt his interpretation contained some truth, but he failed to see that economic conditions were making the workmen susceptible to the arguments of the new leaders. He was no longer in personal contact with the miners, having delegated his routine duties as miners' agent to younger men, and perhaps did not appreciate their frame of mind. It must be remembered, too, that he was now nearly seventy years of age, and that recurrent illness had sapped his customary energy. He was not able to fight the rising tide of socialism and class consciousness that threatened his position and his ideals. What he regarded as the agitation of a few extremists was in fact a mass movement created, in part, by the failure of his policy. His only recourse was to condemn what he could neither prevent nor perhaps even understand.

For nearly a year the conflict between the two factions within the union hinged upon the Cambrian Combine strike, which had arisen from a dispute over cutting prices in a new seam. From the first the Cambrian Combine workmen urged the use of the strike weapon, seeking to involve all South Wales, and, later, the Miners' Federation of Great Britain, in a general stoppage. As was to be expected, the older leaders, and especially Mabon, firmly condemned the attempt ' to redress grievances by this irregular method ', on grounds of principle and because of the financial weakness of the union. Moreover, the South Wales miners showed in a ballot taken during September that they were not prepared to stop work in sympathy.[21] The issues involved were clearly not sufficiently important for the workmen to sacrifice their wages, which, however small, were still larger than any strike pay that the union could distribute. But by November the Cambrian Combine men were in open revolt against the union, issuing propaganda and even summoning a conference of delegates from the entire coalfield without consulting the executive committee. Until the end of the year, however, the older leaders were able to prevent a general stoppage in South Wales, and the strikers came to realise that they would have to associate their cause with some broader issue.

This they proceeded to do by re-opening the general question of earnings in abnormal places. In October 1910 a conference of the Miners' Federation, held at Edinburgh, had accepted a motion proposed by the South Wales delegates that the employers of the United Kingdom be approached ' to secure a fair living wage to all colliers working in abnormal places'. As a result negotiations had been opened with coalowners through-out Britain, although the employers in South Wales refused to consider the matter. This gave the Cambrian Combine strikers an opportunity to win the support of the Miners' Federation, and in December 1910 they announced their willingness to resume working provided colliers in abnormal places were guaranteed 6s. 9d. per day. When a further conference of the Miners' Federation was convened in January 1911 to discuss the progress of the national negotiations the strikers were therefore able to obtain a hearing. At this meeting Stanton and others urged a national stoppage to win a universal minimum wage, as the only means of settling the question of abnormal places in South Wales and throughout Britain. Once again, however, this extremist proposal failed to win support, although the con-ference promised financial aid to the idle workmen.[22]

For the time being Mabon and his supporters had succeeded in thwarting the policy of the strikers and their leaders. But unfortunately for Mabon three members of the executive of the South Wales union were killed in a railway accident while on their way to the Miners' Federation conference. To fill the vacancies caused by their death, and also to replace an execu-tive committee member who had resigned, elections were held in the districts concerned. The result was a serious blow to the conservative faction within the union. Three of the new officials, namely Tom Smith, John Hopla and Noah Rees, were leaders of the Cambrian Combine strikers, while the fourth, Noah Ablett, was a marxist-syndicalist who later became part author of *The Miners' Next Step*.

With such an accession of strength it became increasingly likely that the militant faction would seize control of the organisation unless the strike could be settled quickly. Moreover, the membership of the union was falling, its funds were almost exhausted, and workmen in many parts of the coalfield were refusing to pay the strike levies. Such chaos could only benefit Mabon's opponents, and for this reason if for no other it was vital that he should negotiate a settlement.

But tentative agreements reached in January and again in May were rejected by the strikers, although meeting with the approval of the Miners' Federation. Neither the eloquence of Mabon, Brace and Richards nor the advice of the Miners' Federation could persuade them to accept anything short of a guaranteed minimum level of earnings in abnormal places. The employers' vague assurances that reasonable wages would be paid were treated, perhaps rightly, as being valueless. But more important, the strikers finally persuaded a conference of the South Wales union to adopt the same attitude during May. For two years negotiation had failed to solve any of the problems that had arisen in the coalfield as a result of the Eight Hours Act. It was now obvious that the national discussions on the question of abnormal places had produced no better result. Quite understandably, the general body of the workers chose, in desperation, to adopt the view of the Cambrian Combine strikers that the time had come for fighting to gain a universal minimum wage. Mabon's methods had proved useless, and in the inevitable reaction the leadership of the union passed to his rivals. On 29 May 1911 a conference of the organisation resolved to place a new policy before the branches, namely that the Miners' Federation should call a national stoppage to win a universal minimum wage in the coal industry or that, alternatively, the South Wales miners should strike for the same purpose.[23]

Although this decision to use the strike weapon marked Mabon's overthrow he was not prepared to remain silent, nor was he entirely without influence. On 3 June he published his first attack upon the new policy in the *South Wales Daily News*, opening with the apt and striking quotation from the New

Testament ' the time hath come, someone must die for the people'. In this and subsequent articles he condemned the attempt to bring about a national strike as a ' policy of despair and starvation ' and one that ' cannot but fail'. With a temporary revival of his old vigour and forcefulness, he entered into a lengthy controversy with the extremists in the South Wales newspapers, which drew widespread attention. He could not rehabilitate the policy of conciliation in the minds of the Welsh miners, for their disillusionment had been too complete. But his efforts in favour of moderation were not entirely without effect. At further conferences held during June and July the extremist elements attempted to silence Mabon by demanding his resignation and the election of a new executive council.[24] The motions were declared out of order, however, and Mabon continued to denounce the strike policy. It is not clear to what extent his arguments affected the miners, although it was always difficult to ignore Mabon when he was determined to persuade his audience. But in any case these conferences decided against strike action by South Wales alone, even in support of the Cambrian Combine workmen, and resolved to ask the Miners' Federation to press for a universal minimum wage. The policy of industrial warfare had been rejected once again by the miners ; but this was to be Mabon's last triumph.

With no hope of active support in the form of a strike, the Cambrian Combine committee was forced to acknowledge defeat. The Miners' Federation had withdrawn its financial support, levies called on behalf of the strikers were being ignored, and the strike pay had been reduced. By early August ' the prevailing opinion in the committee was that they ought to go to the men and tell them that they were beaten'.[25] In discussions within the executive committee of the union the strikers' representatives again urged a general stoppage, pointing out to Mabon that the time had come when even he ' ought to put up an unconstitutional fight'. But, as Noah Ablett put it, ' the time for fight has gone by and the time for eating the leek has arrived '.[26] On 1 September work was resumed on terms originally drafted in October 1910.

The Cambrian Combine strike ended in total defeat for

the workmen involved. But its indirect consequences were enormous. The Welsh miners emerged from the struggle committed to agitation for a universal minimum level of earnings. Many unionists had been convinced that the policy of conciliation was no longer practical, and that the South Wales Miners' Federation stood in need of drastic reorganisation. Young and able leaders had appeared, who deemed that the interests of capital and labour were incompatible, and that concessions could only be won from the coalowners by force. Discredited by the failure of his policy, and criticised as lacking the determination and ruthlessness considered necessary in dealing with employers, Mabon's influence was finally broken by the Cambrian strike. The initiative passed to younger men, who were perhaps more sensitive to the changing aims and aspirations of the rank and file.

A ballot held during September 1911 to elect the Welsh members of the Miners' Federation executive clearly showed the workmen's attitude towards the older leaders. Brace, Richards and Onions were defeated by large majorities and replaced by Stanton, Hartshorn and Barker. Stanton was also chosen in place of Mabon as the Welsh miners' candidate for election to the International Miners' Committee, by a majority of 14,000 votes.[27] Mabon was, in fact, ultimately re-elected treasurer of the Miners' Federation in October, and returned to the International Miners' Committee despite the South Wales vote. But he had no illusions as to the significance of the voting. Speaking of the defeated candidates he observed that ' had I been in their places those who voted them out of the position would have voted me out also. Not only that, but my policy, the policy of conciliation and arbitration failing conciliation — a policy that I have lived for forty years to carry out, and also to serve to the utmost of my ability in the interest of my fellow workmen — has been rejectedly unmistakably'.[28]

VIII

RESIGNATION AND RETIREMENT

MABON remained the nominal leader of the South Wales Miners' Federation during the events that culminated in the National Strike of 1912. But between August 1911 and February 1912 he attended no more than six meetings of the union's executive committee, and with the approach of the national strike he finally announced that he would not seek re-election. 'I feel it is my duty to do this', he said ' as my health has been very indifferent and my usual energy has been wanting for a long time, and I now think I should make way for a younger and stronger man. I do not desire to sever my connection with the Federation and hope, in an unofficial position, to do anything I can to support you in your difficulties'.[1]

Consequently at the annual conference convened at Cardiff on 5 June, Mabon occupied the chair for the last time, and read his final address to the South Wales Miners' Federation.

' Gentlemen and fellow workers ', he began, ' the task which I have to perform is one which I do not attempt to disguise causes me no small amount of pain, for I have now to relinquish into your hands the confidence which I have always highly valued and which you have reposed in me for a very great number of years. For forty years I have enjoyed the privilege of being officially connected with the miners of this coalfield, and for thirty-five years of this period I have been allowed to occupy the position of your leader. It is, therefore, no light task to surrender such an honoured position, but I do so with the consciousness that I have endeavoured on all occasions, to the best of my humble ability, to serve the real and truest interests of the men. I do not pretend to say that I have not made mistakes, but I can fearlessly state that, whatever mistakes have been made, they have occurred in an honest endeavour to serve and further the workers' cause, which I have always had at heart. In bidding you farewell as president, my earnest hope is that the organisation with which we are all connected may continue to prosper and flourish, and that in the future it may be even a greater instrument for good to the workmen than it has been in the past. To my friends and colleagues on the Executive Council I wish to tender my sincerest gratitude for the kindness they have ever shown me, and for the loyalty they have on all occasions displayed. To one and all I tender my sincerest thanks. You and your work will ever be in my thoughts and near to my heart, and that God may bless you and prosper your work is the fervent hope of your retiring president'.[2]

When the cheers subsided, Mabon vacated the chair in favour of Brace, the vice-president, who paid fitting tribute to his great services to the union. On the recommendation of the executive committee the conference unanimously requested Mabon to continue his connection with the organisation as an honorary official.

In explaining Mabon's retirement it is only fair to recognise that the strain and anxiety caused by the National Strike of 1912, and the events which led up to it, had undermined his health. As has been mentioned, ill-health had forced him to relinquish his post as miners' agent for the Rhondda district, and also to decline an appointment as labour advisor to the Board of Trade in 1910. Moreover, his advancing years had made it impossible for him to act with his usual vigour for some time past. But in the last resort it was the attacks upon his policy during 1910 and 1911 that impelled him to resign. It is virtually certain that he would not have been re-elected had he chosen to stand, and in any case it would appear that he was not in sympathy with the miners' new outlook. The cryptic phrase *Ti wele hwn paid a gofidio—pawb a gair da*, (Do not be alarmed when you see this — everyone had a good word for me), scrawled across an account of his speech in Mabon's own hand, clearly reveals the real reason for his withdrawal from the union.

Even in retirement Mabon could not be idle. He retained his position as treasurer of the Miners' Federation and of the International Miners' Congress until 1918, and continued to represent the Rhondda Valley in Parliament until 1920, when he decided that ' in view of his failing health he was unable to fulfil his obligations to his constituents'.[3] As late as 1917 he appeared before Bonar Law as a member of a deputation regarding income tax and the old age pension. At Nazareth Calvinistic Methodist chapel, Pentre, he continued to lead the singing with his customary enthusiasm until his death, and preached frequently throughout South Wales.

His main interest, however, was still the world of miners and mining, and he followed all developments in this field with close attention. During the war years he was engaged in defending the colliers against the accusation that they were unpatriotic, a charge which he knew to be baseless. Largely owing to his influence the miners agreed to forego their two-day holiday in August 1914, and he gave his whole-hearted support to the recruiting campaigns launched in South Wales, urging the men to volunteer and make conscription unnecessary. Early in 1916 he appealed to the workmen not to play into the hands of those who, he maintained, were sowing the seeds of revolution under the cloak of demanding the repeal of the Military Service Act. Throughout the war his greatest concern was that the colliers were ' placed in a false position in the eyes of the public by the indiscretion of a small minority who hold extreme views and who manage to gain temporary control of the machinery'.[4]

Meanwhile articles from his pen on industrial topics continued to appear in the local newspapers, which showed that his grasp of such matters had not weakened over the years. Moreover, magazines and periodicals of all types frequently sent reporters to interview him, with a view to publishing accounts of his life and work. By this time his position as the doyen of Welsh mining unionism was recognised throughout the district, and his views sought on a variety of questions. The government, too, had recognised his services to the coalfield in 1911 when, in February of that year, ' William Abraham, Esquire, M.P. for the Rhondda Division of Glamorganshire, was, by His Majesty's command, sworn of His Majesty's Most Honourable Privy Council, and took his place at the Board accordingly'.[5] Mabon, who had previously declined a knighthood, accepted this honour ' because it gave distinction to the South Wales miners',[6] and thus became only the second Privy Councillor to be chosen from the ranks of the trade union movement. And finally in 1918 the University of Wales added its own tribute, when Mabon was awarded the degree of Doctor of Laws, *honoris causa*, at a congregation of the University held at Cardiff on 19 July.

His declining years were free from financial worries, for throughout his life he had avoided extravagance and invested his savings wisely in the tinplate industry and in insurance. Between 1889 and 1910 he had been a director of the London, Edinburgh, and Glasgow Assurance Co. Ltd., a position which presumably made a substantial addition to his income. When this company was merged with the Pearl Assurance Co. he received an annuity for life as compensation for loss of office. He had held over seven thousand shares in the former company, and was allotted five thousand preference shares in the Pearl Assurance Co. at 24s. per share. These, at a yield of 6 per cent, further added to his comfortable income. It is also possible that Mabon's position as vice-chairman of the Miners' Permanent Provident Society carried some remuneration. Of his interests in a firm of tinplate manufacturers at Llanelly little is known, but his other assets included property at Llantwit Major, near Bridgend, and of course his residence at Pentre, Rhondda. No doubt he received royalties for the use of this name in connection with various commodities, such as tobacco, although there is no clear evidence on the matter. And finally a pension of some £250 per annum granted to him on his retirement from parliament by the union made him a wealthy man by any standards.

It is worth noting that when the full extent of his financial success became known after his death it gave rise to much adverse comment. Indeed, this more than anything else served to destroy the prestige and popularity that Mabon had enjoyed during his lifetime. Many felt that no miners' agent should have accumulated such wealth, and in retrospect his conciliatory attitude towards the coalowners was interpreted as evidence that he had ' sold ' the workmen. Those who knew Mabon best and worked with him, however, consider any such accusation groundless. In view of his personal character it is difficult to imagine Mabon betraying the miners, and those who were in the best position to judge testify unhesitatingly to his complete honesty and sincerity. But to a generation that embraced principles which would have been foreign to Mabon it was, perhaps understandably, only too easy to mistake conciliation for corruption.

Weakened by long illness, Mabon passed away peacefully at his home in Pentre, Rhondda, on 14 May 1922, of a heart condition aggravated by pleurisy. Although he was only four weeks short of his eightieth birthday his sight, mind and hearing remained unimpaired to the end. The funeral, which took place four days later, was undoubtedly the most impressive ever seen in the valley. As was fitting in view of his services, representatives attended on behalf of the Prime Minister, the Miners' Union, The Miners' Federation, the Coalowners' Association, the Labour Party, the Colliery Examiners' Association, the Mines Department, the Master Hauliers Association and almost every religious denomination. The collieries were stopped, and the procession moved towards the cemetery at Treorchy through streets lined by thousands of miners who wished to pay their last respects. As Thomas Richards rightly observed, it was, for the last time, truly Mabon's Day.

In considering Mabon's role in the history of the South Wales coalfield it becomes obvious that his policy hinged upon the use of conciliation as a means of avoiding industrial warfare. But this was merely one aspect of his philosophy of leadership, the most obvious of a whole complex of attitudes and ideas. No study of his life would be complete without some attempt at summarising the theories and motives upon which his practical outlook was based.

His views upon industrial relations and trade unionism were perhaps best expressed by himself, in an interview published during 1918.

'I have participated in a few strikes as well as having observed them in all their phases, and for many years I have lost faith in an appeal to force except in extreme cases. The strike is a disturbing element in trade and embitters the relationships between masters and men. There are very few strikes within my experience which have resulted in gains commensurate with the sacrifice entailed. Moreover, before embarking upon these industrial struggles one should not overlook the claims of the public, and especially the women and children, who are the innocent victims of these economic disturbances. All the resources of peaceful methods should be exhausted before recourse should be made to force. Conciliation first, failing which the matters in dispute should be entrusted to arbitration. Under present economic conditions the strike weapon will remain a necessary evil. The remedy lies in the direction of a wider application of the co-operative principle and the fostering of a better understanding between employers and employees. There is at times simmering dissatisfaction among the more thoughtful in the coalfield with the purely wage-earning relation of their industry, and they maintain with John Stuart Mill that to work at the bidding and profit of another without any interest in the work, the price of labour being adjusted by hostile competition, one side demanding as much, and the other paying as little, as possible, is not, even when wages are high, a satisfactory state of human beings of educated intelligence who have ceased to think themselves naturally inferior to those whom they serve. It should not be beyond ingenuity to discover some formula which would lead to a more sympathetic co-operation in place of the hostility which has hitherto existed between capital and labour'.[7]

This, then, was the essence of Mabon's outlook upon industrial matters. But it was based upon a broader principle which embraced politics and relationships within society as a whole. ' His honest conviction was that Socialism, which meant the levelling of all possessions and social positions, was in error'.[8] Moreover, he regarded Communism or, as he called it, Bolshevism, as being the beast with seven heads mentioned in the Book of Revelation.[9] There was no place in his scheme of things for the class war or indeed for any change in the existing organisation of society. He did not support nationalisation or any solution to the problem of relations between employers and employed other than ' private enterprise'. Ideally, he believed, some form of profit-sharing such as was visualised by J. S. Mill, might prove useful. But until that became practical he was convinced that any improvement in the miners' conditions would have to be developed within the existing framework of industrial relationships.

For this purpose he conceived the trade union to be indispensable if the workers were not to be exploited by their employers. It was to be used, however, primarily as a means of defence, as a shield rather than as a sword. Mabon was convinced from his personal experience that the strike was a two-edged weapon, which rarely gained for the men as much as they lost by its use. In his eyes every successful strike was a Pyrrhic victory. Each miner had not only certain rights but also duties, both towards his family and towards the community as a whole. All would suffer hardship during a stoppage, and these considerations had to be carefully weighed before striking.

Since the strike-weapon was only to be used as a last resort, the workmen had no alternative but to settle their differences with the employers by peaceful methods. In this they were to be guided by the principles of justice and reason.

Both capital and labour were entitled to a fair share in the proceeds of their combined efforts. If the price of coal fell, for example, the employers could justly demand a wage reduction since both profits and wages should bear the fluctuations of the market. On the other hand, both should reap the benefits of a boom in the industry if both also shared the burden of a recession.

In a sense both parties therefore had an equal interest in the well-being of the industry, and Mabon's favourite method of demonstrating this identity of interest was by telling a simple parable. Two miners, he would say, once hired a boat at Porthcawl and rowed out to sea, but owing to the riotous behaviour of one the boat was soon in danger of capsizing. When his friend pointed this out and suggested that he should act more reasonably, he received the reply that it did not matter if the boat sank, since it was not their property. Mabon would then leave his audience to consider the obvious analogy.

The foregoing remarks make it easy to explain why Mabon continued to support policies that had been rejected by the miners. The sliding scale, for example, avoided strikes and, at least in theory, gave the men a fair share of the proceeds from the sale of coal ; at the same time it allowed the employers a fair rate of profit by reducing wages when prices fell. In addition, it gave stability to the industry from which both parties benefited, and provided machinery for the peaceful settlement of disputes. The minimum wage agitation, on the

other hand, met with his disapproval, because it seemed unjust
that coalowners should pay a fixed wage to a miner who was
perhaps not doing an honest day's work. Again, the strikers
in 1893 could expect no sympathy from Mabon, because they
had stopped work without giving notice or trying to negotiate,
thus neglecting their duty towards the employers.

Perhaps the main reason for Mabon's declining popularity in
later years was his refusal to support the miners when he
believed that they were in the wrong. There was little room in
the later development of unionism for a leader who could
recognise that the employers were not inevitably unjust or
unreasonable. In the struggle to assert their rights the miners
were not prepared to concede that they also had duties to
perform, and were unsympathetic towards Mabon's conception
of a trade union's functions. While he always acted in what he
regarded as being the men's best interests, a time came when
his ability to see the force of the coalowners' arguments was
interpreted as disloyalty. To a generation that regarded
industry as a battleground in the war between the classes his
entire outlook appeared out of date.

It is not difficult to show that Mabon's advocacy of conciliation was based upon a number of unsound assumptions. The
most obvious flaw in his argument was that it presupposed an
equal willingness to compromise on the part of the employers,
since unless this was the case conciliation could only become
appeasement. There can be no doubt that belief in conciliation
was an article of faith for Mabon, rather than a conviction
based upon logic. It may be noted that the leaders of the
Amalgamated Association of Miners had all favoured such a
policy, and their views must have moulded his thinking during
his formative years. But it would probably be incorrect to
attribute Mabon's attitude solely to their influence. A study of
his speeches over the forty years of his ascendency in the coalfield leaves an unmistakable impression that Mabon was also,
in fact, attempting to apply the precepts of the Christian
religion to industrial matters. The policy of peaceful settlement
and the emphasis laid upon duties as well as rights was certainly
a characteristic of the so-called Old Unionism. But it could also

be justified by an appeal to Christian principles, and Mabon often turned to this source for support of his policies. Indeed, his last advice to the miners, given in 1921, was to ' Be careful in striving for your just share of the lesser things that you do not turn your backs upon the greater. In winning your share of the material, be careful lest you lose your soul. The workman's best friend is Jesus of Nazareth, and it is vain to expect any success of value if unfaithful to His principles.'[10]

Here it must be remembered, however, that the last of the great religious revivals in South Wales occurred during 1904–6. As the power of the chapels declined there were many miners to whom Mabon's attempt to lead the union on Christian principles meant nothing. The growing popularity of Marxist ideas and the increasing number of workmen whose attitudes were not coloured by the precepts of Nonconformity undoubtedly served to undermine Mabon's authority. By the close of the first decade of the century hymn-singing had lost its power to sway the miners, and as fewer men were Welsh-speaking Mabon's eloquence lost much of its effect.

While discussing the influence of Christian principles upon Mabon's industrial policy it is interesting to consider how far opinions current within the Calvinistic Methodist denomination, to which he belonged, affected his views concerning unionism. It is fair to say that this denomination was more uncompromising in its hostility towards labour organisations than any other, and he must have been conscious of this antagonism during his early years. Perhaps it was for this reason that he always opposed an aggressive trade union policy and advocated peaceful settlement. As a sincere Calvinistic Methodist he could take no other course, any more than other members of that denomination could have decided to assist rather than to oppose the Union Clubs in 1831.[11]

It is difficult not to admire Mabon's refusal to compromise with his deeply rooted and fundamental convictions in the interests of expediency. Yet in fairness to his critics it should be admitted that policies must always be adapted to changing circumstances. Unfortunately Mabon showed little tendency to modify his views over time. He advocated conciliation during his

UNIVERSITY COLLEGE
LIBRARY
SWANSEA

later years in much the same terms as he had used in the seventies. Again, he had advised output restriction in 1879, and supported the stop-days of 1900 with the same arguments. His political beliefs remained substantially the same at the end of his career as in 1885, despite the changed attitude of the miners. That Mabon's opinions and policies did not change was evidence of his sincerity, and in this sense creditable. But it revealed a failure to appreciate that conditions in the industry were altering, and also an ingrained cautiousness that amounted to conservatism. In Mabon's case it is impossible to trace the evolution and development of his ideas, for the simple reason that they were not modified to any significant degree. There can be no doubt that towards the close of his active career Mabon was speaking for himself rather than for the majority of the workmen, whose outlook had changed with the times.

Even so, it is interesting to speculate as to the course which mining unionism might have taken in South Wales but for Mabon's leadership. The coalowners were certainly more favourably disposed towards Mabon's type of organisation than they would have been towards an aggressive trade union-ism. They found that Mabon's views on industrial matters accorded well with their own, and were therefore prepared to tolerate some form of organisation among the men under his leadership. Had the early work of building trade unionism been in the hands of those leaders who ultimately superseded Mabon the employers would almost certainly have offered bitter and successful opposition. His conciliatory attitude won the mine-owners' respect and confidence, and enabled the slow work of organising the men to proceed unopposed. When the time came to adopt a more militant policy the union was too strong to be crushed in the way that the Amalgamated Association of Miners was destroyed in 1875. On the other hand, it can be argued that trade unionism as we know it today might have developed earlier in South Wales if the miners had fought the employers instead of adopting a conciliatory policy. Perhaps the workmen would have evolved a powerful organisation under the stimulus of the coalowners' opposition. But all such attempts made in the years before Mabon's ascendancy had failed, and it is likely that Mabon's method was the only possible means of building unionism in the district.

To evaluate the effect of Mabon's policy upon the development of the coal industry in South Wales is extremely difficult, since it is dangerous to speculate upon historical alternatives. Yet it seems likely that the emergence of the district as a major exporting coalfield would have been slower but for the conciliatory attitude which the miners adopted under his influence. By allowing coal prices to govern wages, for example, the workmen encouraged the employers to develop their mines rapidly, since profits would be maintained at a reasonable level. The coalowners' income depended upon the price of coal and the quantity sold, while wage rates were entirely determined by the former. This was an obvious incentive to increased production and, at times, even over-production. Had a minimum wage rate been in operation during the early years it is doubtful whether the coalfield would have expanded its output as rapidly as was the case, if only because its ability to compete in overseas markets would have been weakened. Again, Mabon's advocacy of peaceful settlement preserved industrial peace in the district, which meant that buyers who ordered Welsh coal could feel confident that their contracts would be met.

For these reasons the employers clearly benefited from Mabon's policy. But it should not be forgotten that, as Mabon stressed, a portion of their gain accrued to the miners. The workmen enjoyed fairly steady employment, and wage rates increased substantially during the years of Mabon's leadership. In terms of purchasing power the rise in wages was even greater, in view of the trend of prices. It is true that the men suffered in periods of depression owing to the lack of a minimum wage rate, and may not have received a large enough share of profits. But the overall effect of Mabon's policy upon wages was not unfavourable to the miners. In the circumstances it would be pointless to discuss what would have been the probable course of wages had the men tried to fight the employers and build a powerful union. All that can be said with certainty is that wage rates in South Wales compared favourably with rates in other coalfields until the last years of Mabon's active life.

Mabon's resignation in 1912 was really no more than an indication that his policies were no longer suited to the changed conditions of the time. His views were essentially representative of a type of unionism which had died towards the close of the nineteenth century, and that only remained current in South Wales owing to Mabon's personal influence and ability. The National Strike of 1912 marked the end of an era in the history of the coal industry.   It represented the culmination of a slow process by which numerous local associations had drawn together to form first district unions and later a national organisation. The loose associations that had been forced by weakness to rely upon conciliation had now developed to the point where they could even oppose the government. Advocates of a conciliatory attitude were replaced by younger men, who were more conscious of the miners' power and more inclined to use it. It is significant that Thomas Burt, Enoch Edwards, Thomas Ashton, Ben Pickard, Sam Woods, James Haslam and, of course, Mabon, the men who had built unionism and the Miners' Federation, were all dead or in retirement within eight years of the strike. With their passing mining unionism entered upon a new period, in which its aims, ideals and methods differed greatly from those of its early years.

Yet in spite of the ultimate rejection of his policy it is impossible to overestimate Mabon's services to the Welsh miners. Perhaps the most thoughtful and sincere appreciation of his work was provided by Vernon Hartshorn, who had once been among his most severe critics :

> ' We should indeed be small-minded and unworthy of the movement to which we belong if this clash between the new ideas and the old left any traces of personal bitterness or blinded any of us to the magnificent work which was done by the old veterans, without which we should be unable to carry on our cause to new triumphs in new circumstances. In the days when the Welsh miners had scarcely any conception of organisation on the scale that we know it today, Mabon, by wise and careful work, built higher the foundations of our movement until it was strong enough to bear that mighty structure into which it has now been built. He had to do this at a time when many of the men were indifferent ; when the Trade Union movement had nothing like the prestige which belongs to it now ;

and when the opposition of the capitalists to workmen's combinations was far more deadly and effective than it is in these days.   Only a man of superlative patience, tact and courage could have done the job. Without the industrial power behind him which labour leaders wield today much of his success necessarily depended upon his tact, his powers of conciliation and his personal character. And those powers were such that he became the master-negotiator, the master-conciliator. As time went by new methods were perhaps needed. Industrial power in itself demanded more and more recognition in the miners' struggle. But by that time Mabon's work had been done. It was a unique work, and it had been done magnificently'.[12]

BIBLIOGRAPHY

MANUSCRIPTS
I. The National Library of Wales
    a. Evans, B., ' A History of the Trade Disputes and the formation and operation of the several Sliding Scale Agreements in the South Wales Coal Trade, 1870–1903.'
    b. Davies, D., ' Bywyd a Gwasanaeth y diweddar William Abraham (Mabon)', Calvinistic Methodist Archives.
    c. The Llandinam Papers.
    d. The Mabon Testimonial Fund Papers.
    e. The D. M. Richard Collection (Miscellanea)
    f. N.L.W. MSS. 8159–60. Two autograph sermons of W. Abraham (Mabon).
    g. N.L.W. MS. 969. Abraham, W. (Mabon), Llantwit Major, letter to Daniel Davies, 5/10/08.

II. Archives of the South Wales Miners' Federation, Cardiff.
    a. Minutes of conferences and of meetings of the Executive Committee of the South Wales Miners' Federation, for the years 1908–1910 and 1910–1913.
    b. Annual volumes of minutes of conferences and of meetings of the Executive Council of the Miners' Federation of Great Britain, for the years 1899–1913.
    c. Minutes of meetings of the Conciliation Board for the South Wales Coal Trade, for the years 1903–4, 1905–6 and 1910.

III. Private papers in the possession of
    Mr. Mabon Abraham, Cardiff.
    Mrs. Rachel Williams, London.

IV. The London School of Economics.
    The Webb Collection.

PRINTED WORKS
I. Primary.
    Available at the National Library of Wales.

    a. Abraham, W., *Reminiscences* (date and source unknown).
    b. Abraham, W., *Mabon on the Eight Hours Question* : *being a speech delivered to a conference of the South Wales and Monmouthshire Colliery Workmens' Federation at Merthyr*, 18 *November* 1890.
    c. Coalowners' Association, *Diagram shewing the reverse tendencies in outputs and wage costs*.
    d. Coalowners' Association, *The Miners' Eight Hours Bill* ; *Some Questions for consideration by the Colliery Workmen of the South Wales Coalfield*.
    e. Coalowners' Association, *Memorandum of Agreement made* 30 *June* 1909, *supplemental to an Agreement made* 11 *December* 1905.
    f. Coalowners' Association, *Diagram shewing the fluctuations in the general Wage Rate, and the output per man underground in the South Wales Coalfield from* 1880.

g. Dalziel, W. G., *Records of the Several Coal Owners' Associations in Monmouthshire and South Wales*, 1864–1895, (Distributed only to members
of the Coalowners' Association).
h. Pickard, B., Ashton, T., *The Miners Federation of Great Britain* (Rules,
etc.) (1903?).

II. Secondary.
Arnot, P., *The Miners*, London, 1949.
Coal Trade Pamphlet No. 3, *The Small Coal Question*, London, 1910.
Coal Trade Pamphlet No. 4. *Abnormal Places : How the trouble arose in South
Wales*, London, 1910.
Dalziel, A., *The Colliers' Strike in South Wales : its cause, progress and settlement*,
London, 1872.
Edwards, N., *The History of the South Wales Miners*, London, 1926.
Edwards, N., *The History of the South Wales Miners' Federation*, London, 1938.
Ellis, T., *Thomas Edward Ellis : Cofiant*, Lerpwl, 1948.
Evans, D., *Labour Strife in the South Wales Coalfield* 1910–11, Cardiff, 1911.
Evans, D., *Y Sliding Scale a'r Federation : Drama Gymreig newydd yn cynnwys helyntion
y streic ddiweddar*, Aberdâr, 1893.
Fitzgerald, P., *Industrial combination in England*, London, 1927.
Fry, A., *A Memoir of the Right Honourable Sir Edward Fry* 1827–1918, London,
1921.
Hailey, J., and Davies, C. P., *The South Wales Coal Annual*, Cardiff, (for the years
1903–15).
Hughes, T., *Great Welshmen of Modern Days*, Cardiff, 1931.
Humphrey, A., *A History of Labour Representation*, London, 1912.
Jenkins, R. T. and Ramage, H.M., *The History of the Honourable Society of Cymmro-
dorion* 1751–1951, London, 1952.
Jevons, H. S., *The British Coal Trade*, London, 1915.
Macrosty, H., *The Trust Movement in British Industry*, London, 1907.
Mackworth, M., *D. A. Thomas, Viscount Rhondda*, London, 1921.
Mann, T., *What a Compulsory Eight Hour Day means to the Workers*. London. 1886.
Mill, J. S., *Principles of Political Economy*, London, 1878.
Milne-Bailey, W., *Trade Union Documents*, London, 1929.
Morgan, J., *The Welsh Mind in Evolution*, London, 1925.
The Powell-Duffryn Steam Coal Company Ltd. 1864–1914, Cardiff, 1914.
Rees, M., *Trusts in British Industry*, London, 1922.
Report of the Departmental Committeee on the Miners Eight Hour Day, London, 1907.
Report of the Select Committee on Coal, London, 1873.
Report of the Royal Commission on Trade Disputes and Trade Combinations. London,
1903–6.
Rowe, J. W. F., *Wages in the Coal Industry*, London, 1923.
Smillie, R., *My Life for Labour*, London, 1924.
Stewart, W. J., *Keir Hardie*, London, 1921.
Thomas, D. A., *Some notes on the present state of the coal trade in the United Kingdom
with special reference to that of South Wales and Monmouthshire, together with a
proposal for the prevention of undue competition and maintaining prices at a
remunerative level*, Cardiff, 1896.
Thomas, D. A., *The Industrial Struggle in mid-Rhondda : Some Points in the Case for the
Owners*, Cardiff, 1911.
Thomas, D. L., *Labour Unions in Wales : their early struggle for existence*, Swansea,
1901.
Unofficial Reform Committee, *The Miners' Next Step, Being a Suggested Scheme for
the Reorganisation of the Federation*, Tonypandy, 1912.
Webb, S. J. and B., *The History of Trade Unionism*, London, 1911.
Wilkins, C., *The South Wales Coal Trade and its Allied Industries*, Cardiff, 1888.
Williams, T. M., *Welsh Members of Parliament*, Cardiff, 1894.

PERIODICALS

Anonymous, 'William Abraham (Mabon)', *The International Magazine*, I, 1885.

'Brynfab' (Thomas Williams) 'Mabon', *Y Genhinen*, Hydref 1922.

Davies D., 'Mabon a'r Capel', *Y Drysorfa*, Rhagfyr, 1949.

Davies. D., 'Mabon eto', *Y Traethodydd*, Ionawr, 1949.

Davies, T. E., 'Y Gwir Anrhydeddus W. Abraham : orig fach yn ei gwmni', *Y Cymro*, Ionawr, 1921.

Jones, J., 'The Story of the Rhondda : Mabon, Greatest of the Valley's Leaders' *Reynolds News*, 8 December 1946.

Jones, T. R., 'The Life and History of W. Abraham, M.P.', *The Ocean and National Magazine*, IX, 1936.

Jones, T. R., 'The Life Story of Mabon', *Great Thoughts : a weekly paper for people who think*, 22 June, 1918.

Smillie, R., 'Stories about Mabon', *Answers*, 17 November, 1923.

Thomas, B., 'The Migration of Labour into the Glamorganshire coalfields 1861–1911', *Economica*, November 1930.

Thomas, B. B., 'Mabon', *Y Traethodydd*, Hydref, 1948.

NEWSPAPERS

The South Wales Daily News for the years 1885–1912.

Tarian y Gweithiwr, for the years 1875–1897.

The Western Mail, selected dates as indicated in footnotes.

The Times, 15 May 1922.

The Mining Journal, selected dates as indicated in footnotes.

NOTES

The following abbreviations are used throughout :

C.B.M.　Minutes of Meetings of the Conciliation Board for the South Wales Coal Trade.

E.C.M.　Minutes of Meetings of the Executive Committee of the South Wales Miners' Federation.

M.F.G.B.　Annual Reports of the Miners' Federation Great Britain.

S.W.D.N.　*South Wales Daily News.*

T.G.　*Tarian y Gweithiwr.*

Quotations from sources in the Welsh language have been translated.

I

1. T. E. Davies, ' Y Gwir Anrhydeddus W. Abraham ; orig fach yn ei gwmni', *Y Cymro*, 5 Ionawr 1912.
2. T. E. Davies, *loc. cit.*
3. *Mining Journal*, 3 August 1850.
4. S.W.D.N., 14 November 1885.
5. D. Davies, ' Mabon a'r Capel ', *Y Drysorfa*, Rhagfyr 1949.
6. B. B. Thomas, ' Mabon ', *Y Traethodydd*, Hydref 1948.
7. This quotation is taken from an article by Mabon which has been preserved at the National Library of Wales, catalogue number X.C.T.399. A.159. It has not been possible to discover its origin.
8. R. Smillie, ' Stories about Mabon ', *Answers*, 17 November 1923.
9. Article by Mabon, *ut supra.*
10. T. R. Jones, ' The Life and History of William Abraham ', *The Ocean and National Magazine*, IX (1936).
11. Anon., ' William Abraham (Mabon)', *The International Magazine*, 1 (1885).
12. T.G., 2 April 1875.
13. Article by Mabon, *ut supra.*

II

1. T.G., 12 March 1875.
2. T.G., 9 July 1875.
3. T.G., 23 July 1875.
4. T. R. Jones, *loc. cit.*
5. T.G., 10 September 1875.
6. T.G., 15 September 1876.
7. T.G., 13 April 1877.
8. T.G., 27 April 1877.
9. For further details of the Cambrian Miners' Association see The Webb Collection, Col. E. Sect. A. Vol. XXVI, p. 163.
10. T.G., 28 February 1879.
11. T.G. 1 October 1875.
12. T.G. 6 February 1879.

III

1. T.G. 14 May 1880.
2. T.G., 10 January 1879.
3. T.G., 9 May 1879.
4. T.G., 13 June 1879.
5. T.G., 26 November 1880.
6. T.G., 24 December 1880.
7. T.G., 14 December 1882.
8. T.G., 11 January 1883.
9. T.G., 22 November 1878.
10. The Act contained no provisions for ' contracting out', but the case of Griffiths v. Earl of Dudley (1882) established its legality.
11. W. G. Dalziel, *Records of the several Coal Owners' Associations in Monmouthshire and South Wales* 1864–95, (1895), p. 631.
12. T.G., 23 July 1880.
13. T.G. 23 February 1882.
14. T.G., 14, 28 December 1882.

IV

1. S.W.D.N., 14 November 1885.
2. S.W.D.N., 2 December 1885
3. T.G., 27 December 1888.
4. S.W.D.N., 23 June 1887.
5. T. I. Ellis, *Thomas Edward Ellis* : *Cofiant*, (1948), Vol. 2, p. 49.
6. T. R. Jones, ' The Life Story of Mabon ', *Great Thoughts*, 22 June 1918.
7. R. T. Jenkins and H. M. Ramage, *The History of the Honourable Society of Cymmrodorion*, (1951), p. 213.
8. S.W.D.N., 21 August 1886.
9. S.W.D.N., 13 December 1886.
10. S.W.D.N., 18 November 1886.
11. S.W.D.N., 15 July 1887.
12. S.W.D.N., 10 August 1887.
13. D. Davies,'Bywyd a Gwasanaeth y diweddar William Abraham (Mabon)', Calvinistic Methodist Archives.
14. T. E. Davies, *loc. cit.*
15. S.W.D.N., 26 September 1901.
16. W. J. Stewart, *Keir Hardie*, (1921), p. 45.
17. S.W.D.N., 3 June 1898.

V

1. S.W.D.N., 9 November 1886.
2. T.G., 22 March 1888.
3. S.W.D.N., 13 March 1888.
4. T.G., 12 January, 14 June 1888.
5. S.W.D.N., 14, 15 October 1887.
6. T.G., 13 June 1889.
7. N. Edwards, *The History of the South Wales Miners' Federation*, (1938), p. 5.
8. S.W.D.N., 18, 19 December 1889.
9. T.G., 7 January 1892.
10. T.G., 25 May 1893.
11. T.G., 19 October 1893.
12. S.W.D.N., 12 August 1893.
13. S.W.D.N., 23 November 1893.
14. T.G., 10 May 1894.

15. T.G., 29 November 1894.
16. S.W.D.N., 4 August 1893.
17. S.W.D.N., 27 November 1894.
18. S.W.D.N., 28 September 1896.
19. D. A. Thomas, *Some notes on the present state of the coal trade in the United Kingdom* (1896), p. 31.
20. S.W.D.N., 16 December 1896.
21. S.W.D.N., 29 July 1897.
22. S.W.D.N., 27, 29 July 1897.

VI

1. S.W.D.N., 14 March 1898.
2. S.W.D.N., 5 April 1898.
3. S.W.D.N., 17, 18 May 1898.
4. A Fry, *A Memoir of the Right Honourable Sir Edward Fry, G.C.B.* 1827–1918, (1921), p. 114.
5. S.W.D.N., 1 June 1898.
6. S.W.D.N., 1 September 1898.
7. S.W.D.N., 2 September 1898.
8. S.W.D.N., 14 August 1899.
9. S.W.D.N., 12 October 1898.
10. S.W.D.N., 3 November 1898.
11. S.W.D.N., 11 January 1899.
12. S.W.D.N., 3 January 1902.
13. S.W.D.N., 13 December 1904.
14. S.W.D.N., 2 January 1905.
15. S.W.D.N., 17 November 1900.
16. S.W.D.N., 22 April 1901.
17. S.W.D.N., 28 January 1903.
18. S.W.D.N., 16, 31 December 1902, 8 January 1903.
19. S.W.D.N., 26 January 1903.
20. S.W.D.N., 21 February 1903.
21. S.W.D.N., 15 April 1903.
22. Mabon Testimonial Fund Minute Book, MS. 1252D.
23. S.W.D.N., 29 January 1901.
24. S.W.D.N., 4 November 1904
25. S.W.D.N., 16 July 1906
26. S.W.D.N., 10 July 1906 .
27. W. Steward, *op. cit.*, p. 138.
28. S.W.D.N., 15 October 1906.
30. S.W.D.N., 17 February, 10, 17 March 1906, 14 January, 1907.
31. S.W.D.N., 28 January, 8 February 1909.

VII

1. S.W.D.N., 18 March 1908.
2. *Final Report of the Departmental Committee appointed to inquire into the probable economic effects of a limit of Eight Hours to the Working Day of Coal Mines,* (1907), Part, 1, p. 46.
3. S.W.D.N., 29 January 1908.
4. D. Evans, *Labour Strife in the South Wales Coalfield* 1910–11, (1911), p. 199.
5. E.C.M. 1908–10, 22 March 1909.
6. S.W.D.N., 23 March, 22 May, 1 July 1909.
7. S.W.D.N., 6 August, 15 December 1909.
8. D. Evans, *op. cit.*, p. 195.
9. J. W. F. Rowe, *Wages in the Coal Industry,* (1923) p. 116.

10. S.W.D.N., 24 August 1909.
11. E.C.M. 1908–10, 22 November 1909.
12. C.B.M., 11 January–8 April 1910.
13. S.W.D.N., 5 April 1910.
14. S.W.D.N., 9 May 1910.
15. E.C.M., 1908–10, 15 April 1910.
16. S.W.D.N., 5 August 1910.
17. S.W.D.N., 4 August 1910.
18. S.W.D.N., 13 September 1910.
19. D. Evans, *op. cit.*, p. 35
20. S.W.D.N., 20 August 1910.
21. E.C.M. 1908–10, 16, 29 September 1910.
22. M.F.G.B., 1911.
23. E.C.M., 1910–13, 28, 29 May 1911.
24. E.C.M., 1910–13, 12 June 1911.
25. E.C.M., 1910–13, 4 August 1911.
26. E.C.M. 1910–13, 12 August 1911
27. S.W.D.N., 5 October 1911.
28. S.W.D.N., 10 October 1911.

VIII

1. E.C.M. 1910–13, 6 February 1912.
2. Papers in the possession of Mrs. Rachel Williams.
3. *Western Mail*, 28 February 1920.
4. T. R. Jones, *loc. cit.*
5. Papers in the possession of Mrs. Rachel Williams.
6. E.C.M. 1910–13, 10 January 1911.
7. T. R. Jones, *loc. cit.*
8. *Western Mail*, 23 November 1896.
9. T. E. Davies, *loc. cit.*
10. T. E. Davies, *loc. cit.*
11. A conference of Calvinistic Methodist pastors, deacons and members held at Tredegar on 19 October 1831 resolved that trade unionists could neither join nor remain within the denomination. See *Cambrian*, 26 November 1831.
12. S.W.D.N., 6 March 1920.

INDEX